We are
NIPPON
THE WORLD CUP IN JAPAN

SIMON MORAN

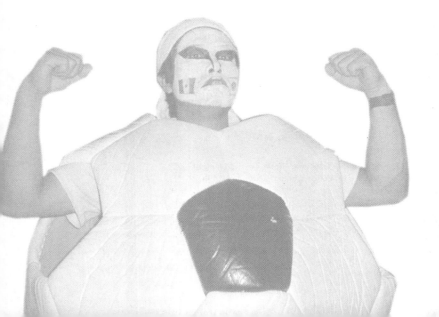

we are nippon

This first edition published November 2002
by S.U. Press, 1-1-13 Ikuta-cho, Chuo-ku,
Kobe-shi, Hyogo 651-0092, JAPAN

supress@japanfile.com

www.kto.co.jp

Distributed by S.U. Press

© 2002 by Simon Moran

All rights reserved.

Printed in China through Colorcraft Ltd., Hong Kong

ISBN 4-901068-01-6

The World Cup made us aware that the world and Japan are diverse. It has given us the opportunity to accept diversity as part of ourselves, to help us build our identities. Thank you, Troussier Nippon, for showing us Japan's potential and diversity.

Funabashi Yoichi, *Asahi Shimbun*

Acknowledgements and Notes

I'd like to thank Takeuchi Koichi, Pak Chong Dae and Shintani Nobuyuki of the Osaka Supporters Club, Alfred Weinzierl and Mayama Hitoshi for their contributions to this book; David Jack, Dominic Al-Badri, Christopher Stephens, Vince Mealor, Randall Smith and all the staff and writers of *Kansai Time Out* and S.U. Press, without whom none of this would have been possible; Largo and Miwa in Tokyo for floor space, cocktails, support and laughs; Andreas Herren at FIFA in Zurich; Jon Watts of the *Guardian* for his help and the volume of good work on Japan he produces; Kyle Barrow for the resurrection; Justin McCurry of the *Daily Yomiuri*; my mother, father and sisters for everything they've ever done for me, and most of all Kumai, who never once complained and offered me her unwavering support, in often difficult times. Cheers.

Throughout the book, where it was felt that an explanation of a Japanese term would interrupt the flow of the text, it has been omitted and included in the glossary on page 189. All Japanese names are written the Japanese way, family name before given name. I have attempted to write without using clichéd reference to samurai, ronin and sumo etc. as they are as relevant to Japan as Round Table knights, Dick Turpin and Cumberland wrestling are to modern-day England. Players and stadium names were referenced by the excellent *BBC Sport World Cup 2002* website and Japanese terms and historical facts by the equally fine *Japan – An Illustrated Encyclopedia* published by Kodansha.

Simon Moran, Osaka, July 2002

Contents

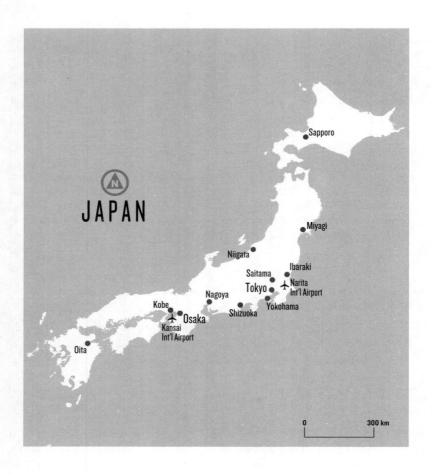

Preface

No country is easy to understand from the outside; yet when you get inside a country the wealth of detail and nuance can confuse even further. Simon Moran has seized the chance offered by the World Cup to get behind the scenes in Japan as they were played out in the World Cup of 2002. Through his keyboard the World Cup becomes a microcosm of Japan interacting with the world, a large pot into which were thrown the Japanese public and those people fanatical or wealthy enough to cross an ocean or a continent to see their nation compete at football.

In this insightful, yet down-to-earth book, Moran, a Japan-based English journalist, allows you to share what it was like to be on the scene. To do this he travelled 6,400 miles and engaged five human lenses with which to view the games. Their conversations and observations relive the feeling and the observations that were made at the stadiums and in the streets all over Japan. Some were disappointed by the results; others by the dourness of football in certain games; but overall it turned into a joyous celebration of the 'beautiful game' with beautiful people. Hardly a hooligan in sight.

Looking to the future of Japanese soccer and Germany 2006, what can we expect? After France won the World Cup in 1998 the Japanese football authorities chose a French coach, Philippe Troussier, to coach the national team. Japan would learn from their European masters. He got them into the second round. Now with the resignation of Monsieur Philippe, they look to the Brazilians, the 2002 winners, for future progress. Their new coach is Zico, the Brazilian who has 10 years' experience in Japan. Japan will learn to play as their masters do. How long before, like France and Senegal, the students become the masters? Probably when the Japanese have learned enough from Brazil and France to develop a style of football that suits their own Japanese culture and a style that comes naturally to the Japanese players.

The title for this book, 'We are Nippon' comes from a familiar Japanese football chant. Japan now has its own chants; its own hooligans and its own exports. What would Japan be without exports? Inamoto Junichi is now a star with London club Fulham and exciting the supporters at Craven Cottage; while over in the Netherlands, Ono Shinji continues to score goals for Feyenoord as they march into the Champions League. He may face compatriot Suzuki Takayuki who has joined Belgian side Genk. With more and more of its star players becoming hardened by international experience, how long before the Japanese no longer have to support other nations at the World Cup and have full confidence in the refrain 'We Can Nippon'?

David Jack, Publisher, S.U. Press

Prologue

Cafu stands on a podium in the middle of the pitch at the Yokohama International Stadium. The first man to appear in three consecutive World Cup finals, he raises the World Cup trophy over his head, his eyes focusing somewhere in the middle-distance, as if searching the crowd for a familiar face. His mouth is agape in shouted celebration and his face cracks into a joyous, wide grin. The podium is held firm by FIFA luminaries. Cafu has the World Cup in his hands and the football world, figuratively and literally, at his feet. Silver streamers explode into the air and the celebrations are showered in glitter. All around the stadium, two million origami cranes float down from the skies.

The yellow shirts of Brazil are victorious and exalted, celebrating. The white shirts of Germany are defeated and limp, slumped on the ground.

In Osaka, Alfred Weinzierl, former goalkeeper with a Bayern Munich juniors team is in tears. He switched off his television at the final whistle. His World Cup ended with him tearing a Brazilian flag out of the newspaper and ripping it to shreds, cursing the Brazilian who stepped on Oliver Kahn's hand.

In Osaka, Takeuchi Koichi, leader of the Osaka Supporters Club, supported Germany in the final as his team, Cerezo Osaka, have a business partnership with Bayern Munich. Before that, Takeuchi supported Japan and England and as Cafu holds the trophy, Takeuchi is jealous. The World Cup has re-affirmed his love for football and for Japan and he swears to support them until they get to the final and he can cry as a winner.

Pak Chong Dae realises the last month has finally come to an end. Pak, a Japanese-Korean, began the tournament supporting Japan and Korea, but ended it as a committed Korea fan. Pak thinks the World Cup won't really have ended if the friendships he made through it continue after all the teams have gone.

In the photographers' tribune, high up in the stands, I try to get a shot of the cranes falling from the sky. I'm trying to take notes and take in the last month of Football Fever that has seen me travel up and down Japan for a month, attending 14 games.

I look out of the stands, looking at Cafu – 69,029 people in the stadium and an estimated television audience of two billion people, one third of the planet, focus on the trophy.

The eyes of the world are on the World Cup.

1

It's Coming Here

Before 2002, there had been 16 World Cups; four in South America, three in North America and nine in Europe. For football fans outside of Europe or the Americas, particularly those in Asia, the World Cup had always been distant.

To me personally, the World Cup has always seemed a long way away. The first one I remember, in West Germany in 1974, took place just after my mother had vacuumed the living room floor. Though this was the first World Cup broadcast in colour, the picture on our black-and-white television wasn't very good and the game itself, to a six-year old, was rather boring. Much more exciting was the trip to Fine Fare on Whitley Lodge afterwards to buy a plastic, souvenir-replica Telstar football. On it were printed the names of the competing teams – I'm not sure if I noticed that it didn't mention England – and the legend, World Cup 1974 West Germany. West Germany seemed a long way away.

In 1978 I had to stay up late watching the faltering march of Ally's army in Argentina. I can't remember if I realised why England weren't playing, but it seemed natural enough to cheer for the Scots. Aged ten, I hadn't heard of Argentina before the tournament started and was unaware of the political controversy that ensured Johan Cruyff of Holland and others' absence. It looked far too cold to be summer in Argentina and it all seemed a long way away.

In July 1982 I had been away on a school trip and, walking home to watch England's final group game, a friend and I wondered whether England could beat Spain by more than one goal so that we could progress to the next stage. We seemed sure we could. Our expectations proved to be overly optimistic. Once again in the front room, as Brian Clough commented that he was sure once we scored one, the floodgates would open, England stuttered to a 0-0 draw and went out of the competition. Spain seemed a long way away.

Come Mexico 1986, when Gary Lineker failed to connect to a second John Barnes cross, my family and several of my friends were packed into the same front room and even my grandmother had jumped out of her seat when Lineker scored. England, of course, lost to the hand and feet of God, and my dad took us all to the pub to commiserate. Mexico seemed a long way away.

In 1990 I was pretending to be a struggling musician, living in a squat in Nottingham. I followed the beginning of Italia 90 while at the Glastonbury Festival, where John Peel announced the scores. Back in Nottingham, when David Platt scored against Belgium, we celebrated by ripping up a bean bag and throwing the polystyrene balls out of the window. Some friends in London got in their car and drove to Italy for the quarter- and semi-finals. I hitch-hiked back home to watch the semi-final, packed into the same front room again. Though this time we got closer to the final, my dad again had to stump up for an even larger commiserating round. My friends drove back from Italy to find they had lost their jobs. I hitch-hiked back to Nottingham and the band broke up. Italy seemed a long way away.

By 1994, I'd given up on becoming a famous musician in favour of travelling the world. During USA 94, I was in the Bay of Islands, New Zealand, working on a farm and playing for the local football team, Bay Cosmos, ending the season as top scorer. England had again failed to qualify and I was again in a different time zone. The routine of milking the goat, moving the cows and cutting the gorse was interrupted by the early rises necessary to watch the games. I wished, I said, that the tournament was being held in Australia. America seemed a long way away.

By the time France 1998 came around, I had made Japan my home. Sitting on the bar in the packed Murphy's Irish Pub in Shinsaibashi, Osaka, we didn't realise for a while that Sol Campbell's goal against Argentina had been disallowed. Just as we had two years earlier watching Euro 96 in the same bar, we saw England go out on penalties. To us, again disappointed, again in another time zone, again on the other side of the world, France seemed a long way away.

That time though, the feeling of missing out wasn't quite so keen. I knew that all I had to do was wait four years and the World Cup would no longer seem a long way away. It would, in fact, be coming to my doorstep.

2

The Bid

Former FIFA President, João Havelange, said in the 1980s that Japan was the perfect place to host the World Cup. This was interpreted by many as meaning that not only was it a good place to hold the World Cup, but that the decision had already been made and Japan would hold the World Cup in 2002.

At the time, Japan was a minor footballing nation where the word 'football' was taken to mean American football and the beautiful game went by the name *sakka*. There was no professional football league, only a competitive amateur league contested by company-sponsored teams and Japan had never qualified for the World Cup. The proposed host's main claim to footballing fame was winning the bronze medal at the Mexico City Olympics in 1968.

Havelange, wanting to spread football across the world, saw similar opportunities in Japan to those he saw in the U.S., another minor footballing nation when it was host to the World Cup in 1994. When Havelange stated his case, Japan was the second biggest economy in the world and had, it seemed, money to burn. Havelange and FIFA were willing to fan the flames, knowing that the potential, in footballing and financial terms, was huge.

In 1992, Japan won the Asian Cup and in 1993, the J.League, Japan's first professional soccer competition, was launched. International stars such as Zico, Pierre Littbarski and Gary Lineker played alongside Japan's own Miura Kazu, the first professional Japanese footballing star. Football quickly became very popular and the stadiums were filled with screaming fans, wielding cameras to take pictures of their new heroes.

Japan had shut itself off to the world from the mid-16th to mid-18th century. Though there were a few exceptions in Chinese, Dutch and Portuguese traders, the outside world saw very little of Japan and vice versa until Commodore Matthew C. Perry, of the U.S. Navy, stormed into Edo (now Tokyo) Bay in the three 'Black Ships' in 1853, forcing the country to open up to trade.

While Japan had been closed, the rest of the world had been through the beginnings of the Industrial Revolution and Japan now realised that it lagged far, far behind. The collective shock was keen and the country rushed to modernise, inviting foreign experts on all matters to educate the country in an effort to catch up.

As Japan was particularly eager to emulate the world's then superpowers, included amongst these luminaries were scholars of militarism. One of them, Lieutenant Commander A.L. Douglas, who taught at the naval academy in Yokohama, introduced football to Japan in 1873.

Away from the football field, Japan's military skills improved and by the turn of the century, Japan had defeated China and Russia in battles, and in 1910, formally annexed its nearest neighbour, Korea, which had often been described as being like a dagger pointed toward Japan.

During 35 years of occupation, that were only ended with Japan's defeat in WWII, the Korean population was subjugated. The Koreans were forced to speak Japanese, take Japanese names and convert to Shinto, the native Japanese religion. The Koreans were made second-class citizens of Japan and subjects of the Emperor, at that time regarded as a deity.

Many Koreans were forcibly expatriated to Japan to work as un- or low-paid labourers and the so-called 'comfort women' were forced to act as prostitutes to serve the Japanese Imperial Army. As far as Korea is concerned, Japan has never suitably expressed regret or apologised for this and the Koreans have never forgiven them.

After the war, the rivalry continued, with conservative Japanese politicians claiming they had 'liberated' Korea and officially-approved Japanese history textbooks whitewashing the occupation. There was a complete ban of Japanese culture in Korea, while many Japanese grew weary of the constant calls for apology and reparation and believed the Koreans would not forget the past.

FIFA itself was not without politicking and while Havelange, backed by Sepp Blatter, stood behind their preferred candidate of Japan, the Koreans let it be known that they would also compete to host the 2002 World Cup. UEFA President Leonard Johansson, tired of UEFA having to constantly back down to the South Americans, supported Korea.

Both countries embarked on expensive bid campaigns, wining and dining the 24-member decision-making committee, funding expensive trips to the would-be host countries and showering them with gifts. FIFA Vice-President, David Will reportedly said the campaigning had reached a 'ridiculous' level and that all that was missing were brown envelopes stuffed with cash.

It became evident that the campaign was hurting everyone involved and Peter Velappen, the head of the Asian Football Confederation (AFC) wrote a letter to Havelange, published in the *New Straits Times* in March 1996, saying that he was concerned about the 'unprecedented rivalry' between Japan and Korea and that the campaigns had gone 'beyond the limits of normalcy.'

Early in the campaigning, Dr. Chung Mong Joon, the head of the South Korean Football Association, said that Japan should atone for its occupation and withdraw its bid.

The inspection committee found that either country was capable of hosting the tournament. They didn't recommend co-hosting, but neither would they recommend which country should host alone.

The AFC realised that were one nation to win, the damage to Asian football would be extreme. A solution was required that kept the World Cup in Asia, yet didn't split it apart.

By April 1996, Johansson and UEFA, at the prompting of the AFC, were ready to support co-hosting and they set about convincing both countries that this was in their mutual interest.

Japan, backed by Havelange and FIFA, was more resistant. South Korean bid chairman, Koo Pyong Hwoi, said that if they lost the bid to Japan, they would suffer 'humiliation for a long time to come.'

The Koreans came to the conclusion that if the footballing powers decided that co-hosting was the best solution, they would agree. The idea of co-hosting seemed the perfect face-saving device and the Koreans quickly came on board and used their representation in the upper echelons of FIFA to make this known.

Johansson used his influence with the executive committee to persuade them that co-hosting was the best option, knowing that this would have the extra bonus of delivering a blow to Havelange and Blatter. It would also make further joint bids from European countries a possibility.

In May 1996, Blatter phoned Okano Shunichiro, the head of the Japanese bid committee, to ask if they would consider co-hosting. The committee sought the advice of former Prime Minister Miyazawa Kiichi who suggested half a World Cup was better than none. The Japanese and Havelange had been backed into a corner, and on May 31, 1996, Havelange announced to a stunned audience that the 2002 World Cup would be co-hosted by Japan and Korea. Then the bickering started.

A committee meeting after the announcement tried to give all the important parts of the competition – the draw, the opening game and the final – to Havelange's original choice, Japan. The Koreans wouldn't stand for it. Dr. Chung refused to be persuaded, fearing that losing the glamorous parts of the competition to Japan would go down as badly at home as losing the tournament itself.

In the end, Japan was given the draw for the preliminary rounds and the final, whilst Korea got the draw for the finals and the opening game. The rest of the competition was split evenly down the middle.

FIFA proposed a single organising committee, though this was rejected by both hosts, who each formed an organizing committee, JAWOC and KOWOC respectively.

The official name of the tournament was another source of disagreement. As the official name was to be in English, the Japanese claimed that it should be Japan-Korea, as alphabetical order dictated. Korea argued that as English is foreign to both countries and FIFA's official language is

French, perhaps the country they call Dae Han Min Guk, could be referred to using the French Corea, which would return the alphabetical advantage to them (over the French Japon).

The title '2002 FIFA World Cup Korea/Japan' was decided upon, though the Japanese side claimed that they had reached an agreement whereby, when writing the name in Japanese, they could put Japan ahead of Korea.

FIFA insisted that the original word order remain and that Japan had to use *katakana* – a phonetic syllabary normally used to make foreign loan words pronounceable in Japanese – to write the countries' two names. This is a snub equivalent to the EU insisting that the British use the words 'color' and 'meter.'

Endo Yasuhiko of JAWOC suggested that FIFA should have made some efforts to better understand Asian culture, or at least the culture of the relationship between the odd bedfellows it had wooed. Japan backed down, but saved face by taking the names of both countries off all official documents in Japanese.

Things were progressing as smoothly as anyone could have hoped. Some even commented that they were surprised at the level of co-operation between the two countries. South Korean President Kim Dae Jung visited Japan and spoke at the Diet, the nation's parliament. He said that there was a new era of co-operation and that although there were things in the past that had soured relations between the two countries, they should put them aside, forgive, forget and look to the future.

At home, Kim eased regulations that governed imports of cultural material from Japan, allowing Japanese films to be shown and popular music to be heard officially for the first time. Despite a burgeoning underground market, this was a significant step in a country many Japanese believed to have been brainwashed for decades by a military regime.

Public discussions had been started on whether the Japanese emperor would make the trip to Korea for the opening game, but in April 2001, things took a turn for the worse.

After the publication in Japan of eight government-approved junior high school textbooks that the Koreans felt 'distorted history', the Korean government demanded that they either be withdrawn or amended. The Japanese government refused, stating that as the books had been approved by the Education, Science and Technology Ministry, they stood by the version of history that had been portrayed.

The row festered and Korea recalled its ambassador to Japan. In the summer, Japanese Prime Minister Koizumi Junichiro, made a visit to Yasukuni Shrine in Tokyo. Yasukuni is the Shinto shrine where the souls of 2.5 million soldiers who died for the emperor and 12 Class A war criminals are enshrined. Yasukuni is a beacon to the far right in Japan and abhorrent to the Koreans and Chinese.

Protests were made and the good work done in the name of co-operation and internationalisation seemed to be coming undone. The emperor's proposed visit to Korea became increasingly unlikely.

In his birthday address in December 2001, the emperor made a stunning speech. He said he felt 'a certain kinship with Korea', as records say that the mother of his ancestor, Emperor Kammu (r. 781-806 AD), came from a Korean royal family. This was the first time a member of the Imperial Household had publicly made such a statement. Japanese nationalists prefer to espouse that the royal lineage stretches back unbroken for 125 generations. The address was front-page news in Korea, though it was not widely reported in Japan.

It was decided that the emperor's cousin Prince Takamodo, honourary president of the JFA, and his wife, Princess Hisako, would represent him at the opening ceremony in Seoul. This was to be the first official visit to South Korea by any member of the Imperial Household.

The ceremony would feature the song 'Let's Get Together', a collaborative effort from Japanese and Korean musicians, with lyrics in both languages. This was to be the first time a song in Japanese had been heard on state television in Korea. The ceremony was addressed by the Japanese prime minister and Korean president and represented the huge step both countries had taken down the difficult road to internationalisation.

3

Warm Up and Stretching

Before the World Cup started, I applied to FIFA in Zurich for accreditation as a freelance photo-journalist, as I intended to cover the events for newspapers and magazines in England and Japan. Having collected letters of appointment from the various editors I was to write for, I faxed them off in the middle of the night. The next morning an email arrived to say that my application was successful. I was going to the World Cup, and I had a free pass.

All around me, jaws dropped in envy and emails with 'jammy' in the subject line flooded in. Applications were hugely oversubscribed in Japan and tickets were hard to come by. Kumai, my wife, said she could see me as an old man in the pub, with my pass as a trophy, hung around my neck. We went out for a drink to celebrate.

In my local *izakaya*, the chef, a keen football fan, almost dropped his knife when I told him.

'*Honmani* – you're kidding? *Rakki yanen na* – that's lucky, isn't it?'

I first met Mayama Hitoshi three years ago when I stumbled into his restaurant on my way home one night. Although the last train makes sure that most drinkers are on their way home around the sensible hour of midnight, there are plenty of places that simply don't shut until all the customers have gone home. Hitoshi works at one of those. Conveniently placed next to the station exit, Mohejitei is a family-run *izakaya*, the closest thing the Japanese have to a pub, where food and drinks are served. Hitoshi cuts an imposing figure in his chef's whites. A high school judo club member of some repute – the reason he claims he's so big and weighs 18 stone – he shaves his head to the scalp twice a year, has eyes that scratch slits out of a bloated football of a face and lips that mangle his thick, almost impenetrable Osaka accent like a huge fish swallowing boiled eggs whole and spitting out the shells.

Hitoshi calls me *shacho*, which means company president or boss, and is a term conferring respect and elevated status. This means he's either treating me well, as any old-time chef would his customer, or he's taking the piss. I suspect the latter.

'*Shacho*, what'll it be tonight?'

One of the things you quickly learn in Japanese restaurants is that most chefs lose interest in you as soon as you think you know what you want.

Asking for the menu is like telling a chef he can't do his job, you either ask what he recommends or let him decide, by asking for the chef's *makase* – literally, 'let the chef do it.' Hitoshi's specialty is sashimi, which he buys and cuts well.

'What's good today?' I defer.

Hitoshi looks slightly perturbed, something I've never really seen before.

'Er, whale, actually. You probably don't want that, do you? They don't eat that over there, do they?'

Muko, 'over there', is the term Japanese use to refer to foreign countries or places other than where they are now. At first this sounds slightly dismissive, though once you get the hang of it, it speeds things up somewhat and sounds almost comforting.

'Over there? Well, not any more they don't. I've never had it, so I'd like to try.'

Chopsticks stop and heads around me turn and stare. The whale arrives, as does all Hitoshi's sashimi, thinly sliced and decoratively arranged on a small mountain of crushed ice, served in a large bowl. As whale is meat, rather than fish, it is accompanied by soy sauce and ground ginger, in place of the usual *wasabi*. I take my chopsticks and mix some ginger in the soy sauce then pick up a piece of meat, douse it in the sauce and eat it. It's delicious.

'This is really good. What kind of whale is it?'

'I haven't got a clue. It's probably from Wakayama, though.'

Wakayama, several hours south of Osaka, is home to several old whaling stations. Despite the decline in the industry and the increase in the whale-watching tourist industry, whale-meat is still sold in supermarkets. The problem for most Japanese when considering whale-meat is not that they see any ethical problems in eating a supposedly endangered species, rather that it reminds them of school dinners.

'*Daijobu*?' The mother pipes in from the till. 'Is everything OK?'

'He's alright. He can eat anything, this one,' the father answers from behind the counter as I eat my second piece, 'Can't you?'

The daughter, who I've never heard say anything other then hello, goodbye, thanks and sorry, smiles awkwardly and busies herself with ignoring me.

Hitoshi has an opinion on everything. He's never played much football, but has an opinion on it anyway. He plays Toto, a kind of Japanese football pools and hopes to repeat the success he had at the horse races one day, winning the equivalent of £5,000.

'I like European football, but the Japanese just don't get it. They're hopeless. They're not big enough. Foreigners are bigger and stronger.'

These are comments the foreigner in Japan often hears. The Japanese often have an inferiority complex towards foreigners when it comes to matters of size and physical prowess. This can often seem like feeble excuse-making, though he does have a point. The average height of the Japanese football squad is 5'10", that of the Belgian, 6'1".

Hitoshi says that he hasn't even bothered applying for tickets as he won't be able to take time off to go and see any games. He'll be watching on the television in the *izakaya*.

I eat up my whale and leave, though not before being challenged to an arm-wrestling contest, which I lose, and making a bet of ¥1,000, just over £5. I think Japan will qualify for the second round, Hitoshi doesn't. I promise to call in often during the World Cup to tell him all about it.

The next day I go to Abeno Sports Plaza, in the Tennoji district of Osaka, to see my friend Takeuchi Koichi. Takeuchi runs a small, non-profit organization called the Osaka Supporters Club (OSC). The aims of OSC are to promote football in the city centre of Osaka. OSC have a small ground in Abeno where there are five-a-side pitches. They also take disabled and disadvantaged children to see J.League games.

Takeuchi is a football nut and cares more about his local team, Cerezo Osaka, than most things in life, certainly more than the Japanese national team. Though born in Kyoto, Takeuchi seems like the typical working-class Osakan. At first a little gruff and imposing, he is friendly, down-to-earth and speaks his mind.

Takeuchi also loves English football, and when his mobile phone, which hangs around his neck on a purple Cerezo Osaka strap, rings, it plays the theme from *The Great Escape*.

I tell Takeuchi the good news about my pass.

'You lucky git. Out of everyone I know, I've got the least number of tickets.'

I had got to know Takeuchi when I did a story on an international five-a-side tournament they had run. He had become a friend and never failed to impress with his extensive, anorak knowledge of international football.

While working to promote football in the city, he had become involved with the World Cup. The club has about 40 full-time members and another 150 helpers and has proposed a 'fans' village' where fans from abroad can meet, exchange information and just hang out.

'JAWOC are only thinking about the 90 minutes of each match, not how it's going to affect people's lives afterwards. There are lots of foreigners in Japan and we have a chance to get together and talk. When the World Cup's over, if people can make lasting friendships, that'll be a great thing.'

Takeuchi echoes the sentiments of JAWOC and hundreds of small organisations for whom 'internationalisation' is seen as an essential thing to achieve, bringing Japan and the outside world closer together, something most people feel is an absolute necessity.

While we are discussing the various merits of holding the event in two countries, another OSC member, Pak Chong Dae, joins us.

Pak was born in Osaka to Korean parents. Though he was born and raised in Japan, his passport says he is Korean. He pays income tax, but does not have the right to vote. Pak went to schools and a university for ethnic Koreans in Japan, and if anyone is in a postion to see any problems or differences between the two countries, he is. Pak will be working as a bilingual volunteer during the World Cup and Takeuchi will be organising events, face-painting and watching games on big screens that will be laid on in Osaka Dome. He is also searching for tickets.

Takeuchi and Pak make me promise to tell them about the atmosphere of the games they can't get to. They also ask me to introduce them to more of my foreign friends so we can all watch some games together. I promise to take them to some pubs where foreigners hang out and to introduce them to Alfred.

Alfred Weinzierl and I first crossed paths when I was writing a story about foreigners imprisoned in Japan. Alfred was involved with a group called the Centre for Multicultural Information and Assistance and has a reputation as being something of an 'Equalizer' figure. He would walk around bars, shops and clubs where the foreign population of Osaka congregate and hand out his name card and mobile telephone number. This could be called if anyone found themselves in trouble with the police, day or night. I was meeting him at Big Man, a huge video screen near Osaka's main train station, and the most crowded meeting point in town. I knew Alfred was German, though he gave me a description of himself so I could spot him amongst the crowd

'You will recognize me easily. I am wearing army-type combat trousers and big boots and I have a skinhead and a moustache.'

I'd already heard about the military obsession, skinhead and moustache. I'd also heard he carried a huge knife and used to be a debt collector for the yakuza. I was going to arrive late.

Alfred was impossible to miss. He couldn't have stood out more if he had been dressed in an SS uniform. I hurried over and made my apologies as he eyed me suspiciously and muttered something about 'typical journalists'.

Alfred worked without a salary and would ask only for his train fare. The interview was carried out in a café. When the waitress approached for our order, Alfred apologised in his fluent Japanese that he had no money and would only take water. I bought him a coffee and a packet of cigarettes and we did the interview, his mood lightening as he chain-smoked and told tales of bailing people out of Osaka Minami Police Station in the middle of the night. The coffee and cigarettes had won him over.

After the interview we met Ikeda Takashi, the lawyer with whom Alfred was to open an office, and Sato Toshihiro, a friend, and went to a snack bar.

Snack is the term the Japanese use for a hostess club and we were duly seated at our table by the head hostess, or *team mama*, and introduced to our lovely hostesses, four women in their early twenties. There was a karaoke machine and form dictates that everyone sings a well-known song, accompanied by the machine and guided by the words on the screen.

Sato sang first, followed by Alfred. Both were greeted with great applause and continued their conversation with Ikeda, ignoring the silent, beautiful women as they dutifully filled their glasses so they were never empty and rushed small, black lighters, embossed with the club's telephone number in gold lettering, to well-anticipated, unlit cigarettes.

To escape my turn singing, I turned to my hostess, Yuki.

'This must be a very tiring job, being nice to people as drunk and as loud as this, night after night.'

In common with radio announcers, elevator girls, telephone receptionists and many young women in the service industry, Yuki spoke with an exaggeratedly high-pitched voice, sounding at once naïve, young, attractive and available.

'Not at all. It's nice to talk to the customers and have drinks with them. It's a good job. The pay's good and the club pays for a taxi home.'

'But you must get some right sleazy old gits touching you up.'

'Well, a bit, but we just tell them that they can't touch and they stop. They're all terrified of the *Mama-san*, anyway, she's really strong and won't put up with any nonsense.'

Though perhaps not the brightest creature in the world, Yuki was certainly charming, she was also a very good hostess, making her customers feel good about themselves. She smiled at me, nodded in gentle agreement with everything I said and complimented me on both my Japanese and my knowledge of the country. In a club struggling to give off an air of sophistication, all glitter, straight lines, mirrors and with an atmosphere reminiscent of a 1980s provincial disco that had obviously seen better days, she glistened with youthful beauty.

Alfred insisted we drink double shots of Polish Pure Spirit vodka, 'The strongest drink in the world.' He then shook a can of beer, pierced it with his knife and shot-gunned it in under three seconds, insisting Ikeda time him on his digital watch.

I was relieved when Ikeda said we should be going. He paid the bill, which came to ¥85,000, about £465. We had been there for 90 minutes.

Since then Alfred and I had become friends and football rivals. After Germany beat England at Wembley, he called me to sing 'Deutschland Deutschland Über Alles'. Following England's triumph in Munich, he didn't answer his phone for days.

I introduced Alfred to Takeuchi and Pak. As the World Cup approached, the anticipation built and when any of us met, talk would inevitably turn to the coming games. We arranged to watch some games together, starting with the opening match.

we are nippon

4

Kick-off – Senegal vs. France

As the opening game is being played in Seoul, Takeuchi has decided we should go to a Senegalese bar in America Mura (American Village), in the Shinsaibashi district of Osaka. A popular shopping and entertainment district, Shinsaibashi attracts a lot of the city's foreign community. In recent years, there has been an increase in the number of Africans running bars and shops in the area. Seen hanging around the streets in the daytime to attract customers, the rumours about the African community in Osaka are no different to those anywhere they are a minority. In Japan, the sight of a black face on the street instills fear in a good percentage of the population.

Our night begins, as do most in Osaka, by meeting outside exit number six of Shinsaibashi Station. This puts us on the *shotengai*, a covered shopping street, next to Daimaru Department Store. At night, as the shoppers are leaving, the street is full of people rushing to bars and restaurants with their colleagues after work. Young men standing in twos and threes, spaced down the street at intervals of about 20 yards, are trying to attract customers to the clubs and bars where they work. Many have extravagantly dyed and coiffed hair, colourful suits and shirts, needing only lipstick, eyeliner and blusher to complete the Nick Rhodes-Duran Duran look of 1984. They approach any eligible-looking young woman that passes. The idea is that after being successfully charmed, the women will want to go with their host to a nearby bar, club or karaoke lounge, where they will be further charmed and drink at exorbitant prices. Those that can pay will do so and leave, probably never to go again. Those that can't may be offered the chance to work to pay off their debt. This could see them employed as a hostess or be hooked into the world of soaplands and prostitution.

Also on the *shotengai* are homeless men, young people selling photos, drawings, poems and false nails. Others are busking, reading the lyrics to their self-penned songs from hand-written sheets on music stands; running electric instruments off generators. There are stalls selling baked corn, *takoyaki* – octopus in batter – and small cakes in the shape of Doraemon, a popular robot-cat cartoon character.

Alfred can't make it but everyone else is punctual. I don't have to wait more than five minutes before being joined by Pak, Will, an English friend who lives in Osaka, and Tomoko, from Will's office. We walk to the bar down Mido-suji, the main street through the middle of Osaka that runs parallel to the *shotengai*. Pak, who said a month before the tournament started that he would support both Japan and Korea, confesses that his loyalties are wavering.

'At the moment, I would definitely have to say that I support Korea, because their football is much, much more interesting.'

Will has already confessed to split or divided loyalties. Born in Iran to an Iranian mother and Malaysian father, although brought up in England and a Spurs supporter, he has a get-out clause ready.

'No one English likes the English, or being English, everyone wants to be something else,' he says. 'The English seem uncomfortable with their nationality, in a way the Scots, Welsh and Irish are most definitely not. Partly because of the violence it brings out in a minority of English football fans abroad. The rest feel guilty by association.'

Will is trying to get an Iranian passport. Every time I've gone to a bar in a foreign country to watch England play, such has been my dislike of the pride shown by my fellow supporters – a pride that so often manifests itself as a hatred of things foreign; a rallying call to the superiority of the English race shouted tunelessly by fat skinheads with necks thicker than my thighs – that I often end up supporting the opposition.

I had watched England's final, crucial World Cup qualifying match against Greece in Murphy's Irish Pub in Shinsaibashi. The regular drinkers – Irish, English, American, Canadian and Antipodean English teachers, financial advisers and some Japanese, keen to practice their English – were squeezed between beer-bellies and shaved heads that had appeared from nowhere. Noting that Nikos Dabizas, of Greece and Newcastle, was an adopted Geordie, I punched the air when Greece scored the first goal, drawing menacing stares from around the room. I went into the other bar, full of Scots and Irish shouting for Greece, and watched the rest of the game quietly. I punched the air again when Beckham scored the free-kick that brought England to Japan.

Tonight's venue, Chez Gaby, promises to be a little more culturally diverse than Murphy's had been, though we are having trouble finding the place. We know it's on the eighth floor of the Blue Angel building, two blocks west of the Holiday Inn.

As there are almost no street names in Japan, addresses are given by a name followed by a series of numbers. These signify an area within the block, the building and the room. Thus, Chez Gaby's address is Nishi-Shinsaibashi 2-8-3-8F-C. Directions can be a significant problem and most bars, shops and restaurants include a map in the adverts that they place in local magazines. We have a copy of just such a map, though are standing in the middle of the street, lost. We also have the bar's phone number.

'What do they speak in Senegal?'

'Senegalese and French.'

'They must speak English as well.'

'Why?'

'Because it's in Africa.'

'Eh?'

'Will, do you speak any French?'

'Um, just to GCSE.'

'Pak, you call them, he must speak Japanese.'

'Why?'

'Because we're in Japan.'

It is often difficult for Japanese to comprehend that foreigners can speak their language. From an early age, the Japanese are encouraged to believe that they are different to the rest of the world, something that has come about as they are an island nation. They are right of course, they are unique; as are the Koreans, the English, the Iranians, the Scots, the Irish...

The Japanese, though, spend the rest of their lives defining just what it is to be Japanese. This difference with the rest of the world is analysed, as are its implications when dealing with foreigners and things foreign. It also comes into play when attempting some form of internationalisation, which everybody seems very keen on. Sentences often begin with either, 'Well, in Japan...' or 'We Japanese...'

It is assumed the foreigner will be ignorant of all things Japanese and must be educated and helped while in Japan. This works two ways. Tourists often remark that they are amazed how far out of their way people will go to help them. Foreigners who live in Japan and have assimilated enough to not only speak the language, but have the temerity to do so, are often frustrated on hearing broken English mumbled back at them.

I don't speak French and don't know if the owner will speak English. It seems to me easier for Pak to do it.

'Pak, just call them, please.'

Pak takes my phone and calls.

'*Haro*, do you *speeku Ingurishu*?' he asks, being Pak, in more of a shout then a mumble.

'*Ingurishu Oh-Kay*? *Gu-do*!'

Pak hands the phone back to me.

Speaking to Gabriel 'Gaby' Dongo, the owner of the bar, who it later turns out speaks Senegalese, French, English and Japanese, I realise that I have been to the bar before. At that time it was being run by a man called Met, a friend of a friend from Sierra Leone, and I had gone along with some staff from the magazine where I work to do a review. We had tried to order from the menu, but nothing on it was available, so we took the chef's recommendation. This was difficult, as one of our number happened to be a vegetarian. The chef didn't often have to deal with people with, as he put it, stomach problems.

The chef's special appeared, and seemed to have come from a tin. Our food writer was not happy, as is often the case when either not cooking him-self or eating in a restaurant of his choosing and, remembering everything he learned whilst living in France, threw his fork back onto his plate after his second mouthful, snorted and refused to eat or speak any more.

The building that houses Chez Gaby is typical of this part of town. Outside there are electric signs advertising 'Massage' and other services for men at prices charged by the hour. Nearby are 'health salons' and gaudy buildings with names like Casablanca, Châteaux Belle and Paradise, love hotels that can be rented for the night for around ¥8,000 (£44) or ¥3,000 (£16.50) per hour.

We are greeted by Gabriel, who stands 6'2" and laughs as long as he stands. He seats us all and takes drink orders, laughing with his customers and flirting with the girls.

'We're gonna do the African thing, we're gonna voodoo them.'

There are around 50 people crammed into the small bar, around half of them African, a quarter European and a quarter Japanese. Some of the Europeans are French and are wearing their team's colours. The pre-match talk is lubricated by drinking and music and when a French girl walks in wearing denim hot-pants with the belt band cut off, revealing her hips and a France strip knotted and tied below her ribs, there is a noticeable jump in the charge in the air.

Chatting to a French acquaintance, he seems fairly confident. I remind him of Cameroon beating Argentina on the first day of Italia 90 and pre-dict the same scoreline, one to the Africans, nil to the defending champi-ons. Gabriel agrees, Pak stretches to 2-0.

I am seated next to Will and Tomoko. She has her hair in short pig-tails and is wearing a tight, white, cotton top, a floral print skirt and sandals and socks, with, of all things, frilled tops. Will is in his customary olive green T-shirt and hat, stroking his goatee beard and doing his best to look intelligent, something he just about pulls off.

We are then joined by Shintani Noboyuki, a member of the Osaka Supporters Club, and his friend Miho. Shintani and I have met several times before, but have spoken little. I have found him to be rather quiet; a little serious. Takeuchi will later tell me that this is because he is *onna-zuki*, something of a ladies man, and prefers talking to women rather than men.

Shintani predicts a 3-1 win for France and Miho a 2-0 win in the same direction. Will, ignoring his fine education, plumps for a ridiculously high-scoring 3-2 win for France, Tomoko a more reasonable 2-1 win.

A Cambridge graduate, Will is on the phone to Philomena, his friend, English teacher and Oxford graduate. She can't find the place, though she is actually outside the building, but just hasn't realised it. Will is explaining.

'No, it's opposite the car park…you have to go inside the building and take the elevator...yes, it does look a bit dodgy.'

Philomena joins us and admits to being more of a rugby fan. Tomoko says she doesn't really know the rules of football too well, but when I quiz her on offside, she gives a textbook answer.

Pak and I discuss the build-up and gossip and Pak tells me Takeuchi will be along at around half-time, as he has to work. Inevitably the talk turns to England and to David Beckham. Miho and Tomoko are agreed that he is *kakkoii* – cool. Beckham is a huge star in Japan, not for his undoubted soccer prowess, but more that he is married to a pop-star, is young, wealthy and good-looking and is, well, a star. I've had enough of all this idolatry though, and tell them he is also well-known for wearing his wife's underwear.

'Eh – really?' asks Miho. 'While playing?'

'Ugh. Image down,' adds Tomoko , showing her bilingual skills. Not quite English, not quite Japanese, but easily understood by all.

'I wonder if she wears his when she's singing,' Pak pipes in.

I ask Miho which other English footballers she likes.

'Rio Ferdinand. He's gorgeous.'

Miho goes on to display more original thinking by saying that she supports Japan, Italy and Spain.

'What about England?' I ask.

'Oh yes, I support them, too!'

The team lists go up on the TV screen and Zinedine Zidane's name does not appear. 'Zidane is dead,' laughs Gabriel.

Photographers from the national newspapers are here and are generally getting in the way, asking people to do poses they don't want to do and poking their lenses in people's noses. Eventually, they get Gabriel and a Frenchman – the girl in hot-pants has sensibly refused – to pose for the camera, holding pennants they have taken down from the walls. They are in the way of the screen as the game kicks off and I make a mental note to never be the sort of cameraman that would interfere.

The game has started, but the camera is only showing Thierry Henry on PlayerCam. There is much consternation. Everybody wants to watch Senegal, though DJ Tony B, a motormouth from Sierra Leone who is giving a running commentary on every move in the bar and on screen, illuminates things for everyone.

'All the French players are from Senegal or Cameroon, anyway.'

I wonder what the population of Senegal is, how it would compare to France. Will, ever the student, gets out his official World Cup guide and tells us that France has a population of 59.1 million and Senegal one of 9.3 million, which, I remark, means it's smaller than Tokyo.

'Uh-uh,' pipes in Tony B, 'Senegal's bigger, but Tokyo has more people, remember dat, it's too overcrowded.'

The Senegalese team had been based in Fujieda in Shizuoka Prefecture before moving to Korea. Their pre-arrival had been fraught with difficulties. Okamura Osamu, the head of the local government's base camp, complained that his workload was too great. He said he had been asked to give the Senegalese gifts of cash and a bus. The wrangling caused him so much distress that he committed suicide, leaving a note for his family apologising, saying he was tired and that his work had been difficult because the way of thinking in Senegal and Japan were different.

Once in Korea, Senegal winger Khalilou Fadiga was questioned by police for shoplifting a gold necklace worth 300,000 won, about £160, as much as David Beckham reportedly earns from his new Manchester United contract in around 15 minutes.

When Senegal take the lead after 30 minutes, with Pape Bouba Diop stealing the ball over the line while prostrate in the box, Pak joins in the commentary.

'They stole that one, too!'

The bar is reduced to pandemonium. Everyone except the French are jumping and singing. Gabriel is whooping behind the bar.

'There's more to come, there's more to come.'

The game kicks off again and DJ Tony B restarts his commentary. 'We're giving you the African quality.'

The ball goes out of play following a Senegal move breaking down.

'That's one of the African qualities, we don't finish what we start.'

Half time arrives and the sound system, the speakers of which we have the misfortune to be sitting next to, is cranked up and issues forth dub and reggae at a level that makes conversation only possible at a shout in the ear.

Takeuchi arrives. He is still ticketless and seems to be going to miss out on the biggest event to happen in his lifetime. More and more internationalised by the day, Takeuchi shouts accented English in my ear.

'*Secondo haafu – Furansu suree go-rus.*' Three goals to France in the second half.

If Takeuchi is annoyed at missing out on the action he isn't showing it. Showing typical Japanese resolve, he says it can't be helped. He hasn't tried asking the British Consulate if they can get tickets for him, although feels that perhaps they should be helping him. The British Consulate in Osaka ran several events before the World Cup, promoting understanding between fans and residents through a meeting at Nagai Town Hall, near the stadium where England will play Nigeria. Afterwards, all with faces painted with the St. George Cross, they distributed leaflets explaining how to deal with the feared invasion of English hooligans. Takeuchi helped at every event, wearing an England T-shirt and, holding an England scarf above his head, told the consulate staff and everyone gathered that in Osaka, England would be everyone's second team.

When Beckham was injured, Takeuchi helped the OSC collect red-and-white paper origami cranes from all over the country. Cranes are a symbol of longevity and are given as a gift to those facing some kind of adversity. The cranes were made into the shape of the England flag to be sent to Beckham to wish him a speedy recovery.

Just as the second half is about to kick-off, Phil, the girl from Oxford who has already confessed that she's not really a football fan, comments on the proceedings.

'It reminds me of that bobsleigh film. That was a sports thing with bright colours, too.'

The crowd in the bar are as tense as they must be in the stadium in Seoul and in bars in France and Senegal. Senegal come under pressure. It is a good opening game, very open with lots of chances. In the Senegal goal, Tony Sylva is playing well, as is Aliou Cisse in defence.

Senegal continue to threaten. Khalilou Fadiga twists and turns Frank Leboeuf then hits the crossbar.

Henry hits the bar for France.

'That's the African voodoo.'

Play continues and the Senegal goal comes under increasing pressure, though Senegal hang on. Every French miss or half-decent Senegal move is greeted with cheers that turn to shouts of hallelujah.

David Trezeguet heads over from an Henry corner.

'Hallelujah!'

El Hadji Diuof attacks for Senegal.

'Hallelujah!'

Three minutes of injury time are announced.

With only 30 seconds to go, Mike is whooping and dancing around the bar.

'Tell the French that they have to speak Senegalese now.'

As the whistle goes the bar erupts into dancing, hugging, kissing and wild celebration. Only in the corner of the bar, next to the toilet where Les Blues are standing, is the scene different. Heads down, they are islands of quiet in the storm of noise and excitement.

I offer my condolences to my French acquaintance, reminding him that Argentina got to the final of Italia 90 after being beaten by Cameroon in similar circumstances in Turin. I don't go as far as reminding him that they lost one of the most boring finals ever seen.

My friend is then interviewed by a Japanese TV crew as he struggles to hide his obvious frustration and disappointment. There is much shrugging and exhaling and we are all living up to our stereotypes. The English gentleman, offering solace with clichés about it only being a game and that there are other games to play, the Japanese camera crew are poking there noses in too obtrusively and the Africans are smiling and dancing, showing the same attractive rhythms that their team had used to beat France. All Africa, it seems, is celebrating. DJ Tony B tells me that all Africa will be celebrating because they are one people.

Days earlier, while watching England struggle to manage a draw in a friendly against South Korea, Will and I had discussed our mixed feelings of patriotism and nationalism. We support England, but shy away from expressing it too loudly. Will thinks everyone has similarly mixed feelings.

'Nobody wants to be English. They're all embarrassed. Everyone says they are English, but...'

Watching the Africans of different countries support their own, albeit from a foreign country, I ask him whether, just once perhaps, it wouldn't be nice to feel that you belonged, to be able to celebrate in being something, belonging to something.

'Well, we had an empire once, they've been underdogs for so long that everything is a celebration.'

Such a celebration that we decide to look elsewhere, it's simply too loud.

As we wait outside for everyone to join us, Takeuchi says he may have a chance to meet Beckham. The British Embassy are going to formally present him with the flag made from paper cranes and Takeuchi may be invited.

'It's improved my marriage, I said that maybe I could meet Beckham and since then my wife and I have got closer.'

Oxford and Cambridge are discussing the game.

'Oh, so France aren't out, then?' Phil enquires of Will.

'No. It's not a knockout. It's what's called a round-robin.'

'Oh, that's a shame.'

'Why?'

'Well, it would be more exciting for Senegal if they had actually knocked them out, wouldn't it?'

We head off to the Pig and Whistle back on Mido-suji. An English-style pub run by a Japanese businessman who used to live in London, the Pig's usual customers are the kind of ex-pats who prefer to live as if they weren't expatriated. They meet there to drink Bass beer, play darts and moan how the Japanese are not ready for the World Cup, how, in the words of one of their regulars, a British man who has lived in Osaka for seven years, goes to the Pig every night and doesn't speak a word of the local language, they 'don't think internationally at all here, they've got their heads up their arses.'

The Pig had recently moved locations after a fatal stabbing on the old premises. It has an unsavoury reputation and the management, keen to avoid it becoming a meeting place for hooligans, has withdrawn all their advertising in the local English press during the World Cup.

The rumours are that there will be ID spot checks on the door. In a bizarre twist of discrimination, foreigners will have to produce a *gaikokujin torokusho*, or a Alien Registration Card, issued by the local government to all non-Japanese residing in the country for more than 90 days, including Japan-born ethnic Koreans and Chinese. By law the cards must be carried at all times. All foreigners without them, indicating they are on a short-stay visa, will be barred entry to the Pig and Whistle, only the local foreigners being allowed in.

As it happens, there is a sign outside with coloured chalk written on a green board, the odd selection of capital letters apparently chosen at random.

'Information

During the World Cup, Customers may be required to produce Identification and be searched. We apologize for any inconvenience this may cause.'

We all troop in, remarking how ridiculous it is, only to have to troop out again as the manager says we aren't welcome because some of us are wearing football shirts. Takeuchi is wearing an authentic Japan shirt, Shintani is wearing a bootleg England 'Owen 10' shirt and Pak is wearing a credibility-enhancing Real Madrid away shirt. The manager only recognizes Japan.

As I don't really like the place or the people that go there, I'm rather pleased, though I of course make furious complaint to the manager, a short man with a bad haircut, telling him the magazine I work for has supported his business for years, that I spend money in his bar.

We go to a neighbouring *izakaya* and the discussion turns to how old everyone is. I apparently look young, but as I am actually 34, I qualify as an *ossan*, the Japanese equivalent of a sad, old git, well past my best. I feel this is a little premature and remind everyone of the well-known saying, taught to me by a 27-year-old barwoman from Kyoto three years ago, when I was 31, as she eyed me invitingly from behind her bar, leaning forward and pushing out her chest.

'Women are good up to the age of 30, men after.'

Just after that she noticed my wedding ring. She asked me, as Japanese women accidentally seated next to me at bars often do, just after I say hello, they compliment me on my use of their language and point at my wedding ring.

'Is your wife Japanese?'

When I say she is, the answer is invariably the same.

'*Ii ne* – that's good – *kokusai kekkon* – an international marriage.'

Internationalisation, the thing everybody is after.

On the way home from town, I call in at Mohejitei to see Hitoshi. It's late and there are only two customers in the place, one of whom I recognize from the train. I'm sure everyone in the area recognizes her from the train, as she stands out a mile with her bleached hair that brushes at her hips and Day-Glo tights that stretch out of micro-miniskirts. Her companion is equally noteworthy, tattoos visibly poking out from his T-shirt sleeves and various pieces of metal piercing numerous holes in his face. Both look like *shinjinrui*, 'new species', the term used by Japanese to describe rebellious or odd-looking younger generations. These days that can include those who bleach their hair blonde, wear contact lenses to colour their eyes blue, green or purple and pierce their lips, noses, eyebrows and belly buttons.

Noting the tattoos, Hitoshi winds me up again.

'He's a Japanese gangster, I'll introduce you if you like.'

I'm introduced to Mikku and his wife, whose name I don't catch. Mikku, of course, is not yakuza, but a singer with a Japanese Oi! band, Strong Blossom. She is a beautician, which Mikku says explains her hair. Mikku also explains his band's approach.

'We model ourselves on the UK Oi! bands of the late 70s and early 80s, but we don't take the politics that far. We don't sing about or encourage discrimination, but we do make positive noises about Japan and being Japanese.'

I am surprised to find such strong feelings of nationalism in Mikku, given his age. Most young people in Japan don't seem to care too much for the flag or national anthem. The older ones who do, stir up all sorts of commotion and mixed feelings.

A certain section of the population delight in driving around in big vans painted with imperial emblems and slogans exhorting the restoration of the emperor as a god. They play ear-splitting, patriotic songs through huge loudspeakers as they drive around cities or congregate outside businesses that are deemed to be unpatriotic.

Another section of the population fervently believes in the national constitution, drafted by members of the American occupation forces after the war. It enshrines peace, denies the country the right to keep armed forces and bans any form of state religion. Nationalism is frowned upon by the left, among whom are many school teachers that are said to teach that Japan should be hated. Others feel that the committee which approves textbooks that can be used in schools is made up of too many from the right, who gloss over Japan's imperialist past.

Hitoshi is unconcerned with these things, as he is unconcerned with much of anything. He sees things in black and white and claims I owe him money.

'Come on, hand over the ¥10,000.'

'What for?'

'What for? We had a bet.'

We do have a bet, but not on the Senegal game and not for ¥10,000 (about £55). I am being wound up again. Hitoshi plays on the fact that whenever I see him, it is late at night and usually early in the morning when I leave, I am unable to remember things with clarity.

'I'm not falling for it. The bet is for ¥1,000, on Japan qualifying for the second round.'

I ask him about the game and how Japan will do in the tournament. He is as negative as ever when discussing his own country.

'With that bloke, Troussier, we have no hope. He's round the twist. Even if we get through, we'll only come second in the group and that would mean playing Brazil. None of the Japanese is good enough. The only Japanese player worth the shirt is Gon, because he is all heart.'

Hitoshi's admiration for Nakayama Masashi, nicknamed Gon for his likeness to a portly television character, is widespread. A Guinness record holder for scoring four consecutive hat-tricks in the 1999 J.League season and the scorer of Japan's only World Cup goal in France 98 against Jamaica, Gon is widely admired. He is seen as having a strong spirit and being ready to give his all for the cause. As *Il Primo Uono*, the English-language, Japanese football website with the Italian name says, like Baggio in Italy and Julie Andrews in the musical world, Nakayama seems to have cemented his legendary status in Japanese football.

If the imperial masters of France could fall to their former colony Senegal, surely Japan must have a chance against Tunisia, Russia and Belgium? Equally, England should perhaps fear Sweden more than Argentina. England could play Japan in the semi-final in Osaka, only 40 minutes from my house. England could then carry the Japanese hopes along with them, beat Brazil in the semi-final and crush the Germans in the final.

The madness and the dreaming have started. The endless possible permutations will be re-evaluated with each goal scored, disallowed or offside given. Each country will take pride in the performance of its players, who each carry the hopes of their nation onto the pitch.

The supporters will be representing their country too. How will Mikku's nationalism fare when up against that of the English right, if any of them get through the net laid out to catch them?

How many will attempt some form of internationalisation?

Is it possible to be both patriotic and international?

Will Korea and Japan form some kind of positive relationship or get bogged down in petty squabbling and one-upmanship?

Will the football be any good?

The World Cup has kicked off.

we are nippon

5

Safety in Saitama – England vs. Sweden

After a quiet friendly against Cameroon in Kobe – where thousands of Japanese wearing England shirts turned up to watch their heroes, but didn't know what to sing – England's first game proper is against Sweden at Saitama Stadium, about 20 miles north from the centre of Tokyo.

Saitama is no exception to the national mood, and locals have formed a 400-strong 'vigilance committee' to patrol streets and protect children from any possible harm. Shopkeepers have closed the shutters on their premises for the day.

At one o'clock in the afternoon on the train out of Tokyo's Nagata-cho Station on the Namboku Line, all seems eerily quiet. Though the train is be-decked in FIFA posters, some showing the past winners from 1966 through to 1990, there is little evidence to suggest that the World Cup is about to start in the Kanto, the capital region of Japan.

Ten minutes into the journey, a family of four Japanese get on the train. Three of them are wearing England sweatbands and they all get their tickets out of the clear plastic official FIFA WORLD CUP™ ticket holders they wear around their necks and begin checking them. Here, at last, are some fans.

Another ten minutes and a Japanese man wearing a Newcastle shirt gets on. I turn to him and say it's a shame that Alan Shearer has retired from international football. Fuji Yoshihiko then displays a detailed knowledge of the minutiae of the Premier League and England's international career to date, not at all uncommon with the Japanese football fanatic.

'It is a shame about Shearer,' he agrees, 'and Heskey is a bit of a lump, but if Dyer is fit and can get a game, England might do quite well. I wish the English wouldn't stick so rigidly to 4-4-2, though, it's a bit limiting.'

Quite naturally, given his colours and opinions, I assume Mr. Fuji is supporting England.

'That's right, I'm supporting England – and Sweden.'

Mr. Fuji is not alone in his divided loyalties. Many Japanese, in common with Miho in the bar whilst watching the opening game, have taken on at least a second team, if not a third, fourth and fifth. Divided loyalties don't seem to be a problem, it all seems to be in the spirit of things international. The fear of trouble, though, is real enough.

we are nippon

'I'm a bit worried about hooligans, but I think everything will be OK. I hope so.'

As the train moves on toward Urawa Misono, the station nearest the stadium, more and more England fans, wearing England tops, England T-shirts, England flags, scarves, wigs and with painted faces, all of them Japanese, get on the train. I am the only foreigner until Akabane Iwabuchi, about 20 minutes from Urawa, where some real-life English fans, recently arrived from the great overseas, get on. Decidedly taller and pastier than the fans on the train, they have trademark beer bellies that they are adding to from cans of beer. Their whiteness adds some colour to the train.

All eyes turn to them, most not really knowing what to make of these visitors from a country they feel some sort of connection to. The English fans are equally bemused by the sight of what greets them on the train. Japanese-England fans display, wear and paint themselves in the colours of their adopted team. The English-England fans don't.

There is a heavily pregnant pause, before a young Japanese boy speaks.

'*Haro*!'

'*Kon-nichi wa-ah*!'

'Where you *comu furomu*?'

'En-ger-lund!'

'*Ingurando*! Yeah!'

'England. Yesssssss!'

The ice broken, thumbs jerk upwards, photographs are taken and peace signs given. Disarmed by an inability to communicate properly, everyone resorts to a kind of international sign language they know will be understood; handshakes, bows and smiles and words spoken loudly in a form of broken English. If this small exercise in internationalisation is anything to judge by, everything will be just fine.

Arriving at the station, the train is packed, and though still mostly Japanese, a larger contingent of English supporters are now on the train. As the doors open and people go up the escalators, they are greeted by a sea of people. Women wearing kimono hand out leaflets produced by the Urawa-Saitama Supporter's [sic] Network. 'Welcome!' it screams. Written in English, the booklet is a guide to trains, toilets, money and the seasons. There is a section entitled 'The Wisdom in Daily Life', pointing the new arrival to discount shops and free Internet access and a section called, 'The secret to becoming good friends with Japanese people'. This section suggests a couple of pantomime-style, action gags supporters can try to make new friends and then explains some possible rudeness the visitor may come across.

'The morning rush hour in Japan is hell. Moreover, many people are in a bad mood and in a hurry. When they bump into you, they don't apologize. That's because it's so crowded, you cannot avoid bumping into people. People don't see any need to apologize for the inevitable.'

36

It also suggests holding open doors for women, as Japanese men don't usually do this.

Swedish supporters dressed as Vikings go one way, Japanese flying the English flag the other. Outside the ticket gates, heavy Scouse accents like those heard outside any concert or sport event in England, offer to buy or sell.

'Tickets, any tickets?'

Tickets are on sale for ¥60,000 (about £325), but very few are buying. Young Japanese fans hold cardboard signs above their heads with hand-written messages in Japanese and English asking for spare tickets. Most say they won't pay more then ¥25-30,000.

A group of young England fans unfurl their flag, telling me they have never experienced anything like this before, being here where nobody understands a word you say. George, the most animated, possibly most drunk of the group, Cross of St. George sunglasses perched on the top of his head, says he is having a brilliant time, though he appears a little bewildered by being so obviously out of his normal environment.

'It's just like...well, *it is* a foreign country, innit?'

Down the stairs leading from the station, more signs are held up by fans wanting tickets. A large concourse stretches over to a few shops and people mingle, taking photographs of each other, exchanging more handshakes and bows. There is an excited, confused atmosphere of anticipation.

The walk from the station to the stadium is a long one. As the rehearsal of the national anthems is heard from the stadium, the path crawls past fields of vegetables, some with CDs on string, gently listing in the breeze, flashing and acting as scarecrows.

The stadium has been built in the middle of nowhere and turning a corner, it stands, like a message from the future, rising incongruously from a newly-planted paddy field with irrigation channels dug in a style unchanged for centuries.

Purpose-built for football with a capacity of 63,700, the stadium has silver roofs curving over the two main stands, two large screens for replays, eleven elevators, is earthquake-proof to 7.2 on the Richter Scale and collects rainwater from the roof, which is used to water the pitch and flush the toilets. In case of natural disasters, the water can be purified and stored. All the electricity needed for non-match, day-to-day running is supplied by solar panels on the roof.

I approach an elderly man wearing long black boots, a white shirt and brimmed sun-hat who has stopped working in one of the fields and is looking incredulously at the procession of painted people going past. I ask him what he thinks of the magnificent stadium, of this fantastic event, the World Cup and all these marvellous visitors from all over the world.

He gets on his bicycle and rides away.

I get a good look at three sides of the stadium as I have to walk around it to get to the media centre. Once there, sweating, I pick up my ticket, which is for the pitch, and make my way to the photographers' briefing, a compulsory event.

Having been buoyed by the goodwill on the train, outside the station and on the way to the stadium, I quickly lose a little faith in my fellow countrymen. A large group of English photographers has commandeered the seats in the centre of the room. All of them are wearing shorts and most have shaven heads. With their dirty shoes up on the chairs and the camaraderie of a group of Club 18-30 holidaymakers in Majorca, they swap jokes about tits, cocks and farting, which one of them delights in lifting his right buttock from his seat and doing, much to his friends' amusement. They seem like a group of immature, overweight, balding schoolchildren on a school-trip to the park on the first day of summer. I want neither to be associated with their nationality nor their profession.

I make my way out onto the pitch.

When the teams come out to warm up there is a huge roar. In contrast to the friendly at Kobe, the English are making a lot of noise and the Japanese are joining in. There are small pockets of yellow amongst a stadium that is painted in broad strokes of red and white. England are at home.

There are rows and rows of empty seats. A ticketing problem has meant that 8,000 seats are unsold and outside the ground, fans without the money or will to pay touts for tickets are yelling in frustration as they can see the empty seats from outside. The touts are equally frustrated and, not wanting to lower prices for the upcoming Argentina game, rip up their unsold tickets.

The day before, FIFA had put 2,500 tickets up for sale on its website, only for the huge demand to cause the system to crash, meaning no tickets could be sold.

Those lucky enough to be in the stands can now see Robbie Fowler, Paul Scholes, Joe Cole, Teddy Sheringham and Sammy Lee knock balls around. Standing behind the advertising hoardings next to the goal, only a few feet away from them, the speed and strength of the passing and the skill with which they nonchalantly flick the ball to each other is impressive. Ray Clemence leads the goalkeepers in some practice and David James approaches the advertising hoardings I'm standing behind to collect some errant balls.

He is huge. Standing eight inches taller then me, the muscles stand up on his shoulders from underneath his jersey. He notices me staring.

'Hello. How are you?'

'Er, fine. You?'

'Fine, thanks.'

It's my turn to feel like a schoolboy.

Sheringham, Fowler and Cole take shots in at David Seaman. The balls are flying ferociously into the photographers' section and parts of the crowd behind the goal. All of a sudden this is not a safe place to be. One shot goes wide and over the goal and screams into the crowd, catching a middle-aged England fan directly in the face. He drops like a beer barrel descending the chute to the cellar. When he staggers to his feet, he is visibly in pain, his face white and blood dripping from his nose.

Another ball lands at my feet. Clemence is collecting balls on the other side of the hoardings. Rolling the sole of my foot over the top of the ball, I bring it backwards and move my foot to the bottom of the ball to then flick it deftly into Clemence's arms. The ball trundles pathetically along the ground and hits the back of the hoarding. Clemence grimaces and his eyes roll, like an enthusiastic P.E. teacher saddled with an uncoordinated pupil.

'It's my shoes,' I protest as I pick the ball up and hand it to him.

The teams disappear back into the changing rooms and the noise level steadily rises.

The photographers all line up at the side of the pitch and wait to be taken down to the tunnel. Guided as a pack behind a rope, there is a lot of pushing and shoving until the ropes disappear and everyone makes a mad dash for the best shooting position they can get. Some wait opposite where the teams will line up for the national anthems, the rest form lines between the pitch and the tunnel where they will emerge. The teams file out to the World Cup 'Anthem' by Vangelis and line up opposite the dugouts. Sven-Goran Eriksson sings neither the English nor Swedish national anthem.

The English fans sing theirs badly, getting the timing all wrong, and then boo the Swedes.

Each player is accompanied by a child wearing a bright yellow T-shirt and bright red shorts. The T-shirt says, 'Say Yes For Children' and is sponsored, quite naturally, by Adidas, one of the 'official partners of the 2002 FIFA World Cup Korea/Japan™' and carries the World Cup™ Logo©. The children stand with the players while the national anthems are sung. A voiceover follows, first in English, spoken by a non-native female speaker with an exaggerated, high-pitched voice and the cloying false enthusiasm of an announcer on the Disney Channel, then in Japanese by a man who manages to sound more like a human being. The voiceover thanks FIFA for dedicating the 2002 World Cup™ to children and urges the crowd to, 'Say yes for children. Please give the children a huge round of applause.'

The children leave the field to a muted reception.

At kick-off, there is a blanket of flashlights around the stadium and a huge roar. The flashes and roar increase in volume after a few moments when Beckham gets his first touch.

On five minutes the crowd breaks into a chorus of 'Rule Britannia'. With 'God Save the Queen' and this imperial masterpiece, the English revel in their imperial Britishness. There are very, very few Union flags on display and while the crowd at England matches now seems to take pride in their country, not the union, there are no songs for them to express this re-defined patriotism. Perhaps they could try 'Jerusalem' or 'There'll Always be an England', though I wonder how many know the words.

I'm shaken from my wonderings by a FIFA official who tells me to sit down. Not having the equipment to justify being where I am, I decide to make my way up into the photographers' tribune up in the stands. I sprint up the five flights of stairs, fearing that I'll miss a goal.

The early exchanges are aerial and neither team looks particularly com-fortable on the ball. England looking to set Michael Owen or Darius Vassell away, having slightly the better of the opening 20 minutes.

On 24 minutes, the ball goes out for an England corner on the far side. David Beckham strolls over, his Mohican standing firm. As he swings to kick, the stadium lights up with the flashes of thousands of souvenir photographs.

Sol Campbell jumps to meet the ball, which flies at a terrific speed past Magnus Hedman. The stadium explodes as on the pitch the play-ers congratulate first Campbell then Beckham, the real hero for most of the crowd.

To complement the style of play so far, the crowd adapts the old Arse-nal favourite.

'One-nil, to the En-ger-land!'

Sung to the tune of Village People's 'Go West', a rallying cry to the gay community of America to move to California.

'One-nil, to the *En-ger-land*!'

The game continues with both teams playing more on the floor and each trying to get forward. Sweden go close with Erik Larsson, England with Ashley Cole and then Sweden again with Marcus Allback.

The crowd begins another chorus of 'Rule Britannia', or rather the only two lines that they know, missing out the opening divine call for Brit-ain to rule the world. The song doesn't last long and the game goes a little flat. The crowd, though, do get another photo opportunity as Beckham takes another corner just before the half-time whistle.

After a half-time beer, the fans settle into singing the theme from *The Great Escape*, presumably refusing to stay prisoner to the Germans for much longer. Though beers are only supposed to be sold one per fan, many simply get round this by buying three or four, 'for friends.' Spirits are cer-tainly high at the beginning of the second half.

The high spirits soon wane as England come under repeated Swedish attack. The Swedes don't really make the most of the opportunities they have. Rio Ferdinand is unpunished for a push in the box and Danny Mills is having trouble on the right. Seaman makes a save and the Swedish con-tingent in the crowd begin to make themselves heard. England panic a little.

On 59 minutes, Mills attempts to chest the ball back to Seaman. He fails and can't recover from his mistake, only clearing the ball to Niclas Alexandersson, who buries it.

1-1.

Two minutes later, it's almost 2-1 to Sweden as Seaman saves from Lucic.

Beckham goes off on 63 minutes, replaced by another partially-fit player, Kieron Dyer. England come under attack again and are under the cosh until Owen, so far anonymous, drags a shot just wide of Hedman's right-hand post.

England cannot seem to find any rhythm and resort to playing long balls, looking for Emile Heskey, which suits the tall Swedish defenders.

After a promising first half, England do not look very good and the crowd is quiet. In the last ten minutes the English defence look decidedly nervous, whilst the Swedes, who seem to be happy to play for a draw, knock it about well at the back.

Both teams miss half chances and after four minutes of time added on, the whistle blows, sparing the crowd any more boredom.

On the way out, two large England fans are talking. They are really angry at the result, at the Swedes for having the gall to equalise and outplay England in the second half. Really, really angry. They are shouting obscenities and the veins stick out on their necks. Somebody will have to pay.

Further down the steps, the queue has slowed and they seem to have calmed down a little. At the bottom of the stairs, the volunteer staff line the exits to send the spectators on their way.

'*Otsukare sama deshita* – thanks for your hard work!'

'*Omedeto gozaimasu* – congratulations!'

'Thank you! Goodbye! Please come back soon!'

The two fans don't know what to make of it. They shake hands with the staff and meekly make their way outside to join the queue for the shuttle buses.

'Ah well, maybe not, then. How could you cause any bother for people as nice as that?'

Outside the stadium there is no trouble at all. The crowd disperse fairly quietly, subdued by an uninteresting match.

After the queues for the buses have gone, everyone has disappeared, some to Roppongi, Tokyo's famous entertainment district, others to local bars and restaurants or back to their hotels or houses. Back in Saitama, the locals are left wondering what all the fuss was about. The English fans in particular are commended on their gentlemanly behaviour. The manager of a bar near the stadium says that his office had sent security guards, who, having nothing to do, soon left. The only real complaint comes from a local resident, who said that there were too many police, that they made their presence felt in the wrong way and had spoiled the atmosphere, which was a bit oppressive.

All seems well. After a few drinks with some friends, we make our way back to Tokyo. We discuss how bad England were and that there are always unrealistic expectations whenever they play in an international tournament. We had, after all, just played Sweden, hardly an international giant and we still haven't beaten them since 1968. The next game is against Argentina, who, my friend says, have brilliant players, loads of them.

The late television news interviews a couple of nervous Swedes in Roppongi who say they wouldn't be wearing their colours if England had lost. The streets are crowded with merrymakers, many of them very obviously drunk, most of them Japanese. The police hold signs in the air that say, 'Be Quiet' and 'Please Move On'. Some fans in Sweden and England shirts laugh and put there index fingers to their pursed lips.

'Ssshhhh!'

In the morning the *Mainichi Daily News* website has some bad news. Over-excited fans have scuffled with police. There they are in full colour, hooligans in England shirts fighting with the police – all of them Japanese.

6

Getting the Point – Japan vs. Belgium

I have the mother of all hangovers. Thankfully the trip to the stadium is the same one as I made two days ago, and though I do my level best to cock it up, in my stupor I stumble on auto-pilot onto the three different trains that are necessary and arrive, much, much later than planned, at Urawa Misono Station.

The scene on arrival forces more than a little life into me. If the sense of excitement and anticipation before the England game was keen, today it's razor sharp, and rather than me being able to cut the atmosphere, it slices into me. Simply, the buzz rings round the station, outside and all the way up the path to the stadium.

Today is a day like no other: Japan's first home game in the World Cup.

The queues in the station to buy return tickets stretch outside the station building. It is hot and smells of excited, sweating humanity. I go into the station master's office and buy a ¥3,000 pass from him directly instead of queuing at the machines and am on my way in a jiffy, down the stairs, leaving girls in summer kimono in the queue, complaining about the heat.

Outside, fans with no tickets hold up cardboard signs asking for some. Tickets are said to be changing hands for over ¥120,000, about £650.

The goodwill of two days ago continues and Belgian fans, dressed as Red Devils with all exposed skin painted red and carrying inflatable tridents, stab Japan fans in blue, wearing headbands printed with the Japanese flag and 'Victory at all costs!'

Some wear football hats, only their faces poking from a 1970s style black-and-white, hexagonal football. Others carry dolls for good luck; some have their faces painted with the orb of the Hinomaru, the Japanese flag, others with the rising sun – the flag of the old imperial Japanese navy and the current Maritime Self-Defence Force. Belgians wear jester-style hats in red, black and yellow and Japanese girls reindeer horns in red and white.

Everyone is asking everyone else if they can take their photo, or have one taken together. Nobody minds; everybody is happy. What little communication can be made is being done so very well.

Walking up the path to the stadium a girl has the Hinomaru wrapped around her waist, her backside bobbing left and right in the red of the sun. A toddler in a pushchair holds a JFA flag; kids wear Japan shirts, shorts and hats and carry Japan rattles, their faces painted with the national flag, their mothers smiling down indulgently.

The stadium again stands dominant amongst the fields and girls pose coyly for their photo to be taken in front of it. Two fans arrive in one giant Japan shirt, both their heads emerging from its neck as it reaches down around their feet.

'It's hot! It's hot!'

A small price to pay to show your support and perhaps get your face in the papers or on television.

A group of Belgians pour from a coach, the fighting poses they strike at odds with their mouse-like make-up and balloons on their heads.

The queues stretch long and orderly. No one complains. I think I've missed the photographers' briefing when I arrive at the media centre, which I confirm by asking a Frenchman wearing a red photographer's bib.

'The briefing finished a long time ago.'

'Did they say anything important?'

'I don't know, because I didn't go to there.'

I had been worried that perhaps I would have my ticket withheld or have to suffer some other punishment, like standing in the corner facing the crowd for the first half, but it seems I am the only one worried, I'm the only one taken in by FIFA's matronly stance. The rest of my colleagues couldn't seem to give a toss about much until the action starts, after which, beware the elbows.

The cynicism continues as I attempt to repair my hangover with several cups of 'special coffee' from the media centre cafeteria menu. I sit at a table near the same English photographers I recognize from the England vs. Sweden game. One of them is showing off the photographs he had taken of mini-skirted high-school girls on the subway trains since arriving. He thinks he may be able to sell them when he gets home. Today's banter consists of more objectification of their hosts, this time concerning their size and whether a good shooting position will be found when the teams come out of the tunnel.

'Well, these Japs are so small, that, even if you don't get there before them, you can stand behind them and shoot over their heads, can't you?'

'You could sit down behind them and still shoot over their heads, couldn't you?'

'Anyway, they ain't gonna be pushing in, are they? They're all too polite.'

Obviously at a loose end, they go on to analyse the lyrics of The Vapors' 'Turning Japanese', a song about loneliness, boredom and masturbation.

Whether they are about to make the change themselves or not, I'm less than enamoured of my countrymen again. They have a bit of a shock coming, though, I silently console myself. They obviously didn't pick up a Urawa-Saitama Supporter's Network's *Welcome Guide*. At least one of their stereotypes is about to be comprehensively shattered, and there will be no need to apologise.

Out on the pitch, the players are already out and warming up. The volunteer staff are standing behind a line they cannot cross that leads out on the pitch, craning their necks to get a glimpse of their heroes.

The crowd is notable for the number of women and children that are in it. It is a real family day out; everybody wants to be a part of it and many are dressed for the occasion. One man's head is completely obscured by the outsized Fevernova football he is wearing on it. Down near the corner flag, none other than Buddha takes in the warm-up and stretching. Next to him, a samurai looks on.

One group wears identical T-shirts trying to influence Troussier's selection. 'We need Gon!'

FIFA, meanwhile, has some important announcements to make.

'Today's National Team Flag Bearers have been selected by Coca-Cola!'

'The FIFA Fair Play Flag Bearers have been chosen by Adidas!'

'The Junior Field Cameramen are brought to you by Fuji Film!'

'The player escorts today have been selected by McDonald's!'

Banners and flags are strung over the walls in front of the stands. Many have messages of good luck scrawled in a mixture of Japanese: 'Let's enjoy the World Cup', 'Cause a Japanese Sensation!'; English: 'Do your best!', 'Proud of you!'; and Italian: 'Verdista'.

Some official stadium signs in English urge the team on.

'Get the Dream! Get 2002!'

The crowd take photos and videos, one man using his laptop to do so. A huge Japan shirt is passed over the heads of the crowd, followed by a huge Japanese flag, daubed with names and more messages of good luck.

This is followed by a Mexican wave with a twist; as each person stands up and puts their arms above their head, they hold the hand-drawn paper Hinomaru flag that was waiting for them on their seat when they arrived. This is not just crowd participation, it is crowd nationalism of an international, footballing kind. It looks fantastic.

The team announcements are made, each player's face appearing on the large screens at either end as his name is called. Huge cheers greet each Japanese player's name, the crowd going mad when they hear the name of Nakata Hidetoshi, Japan's brightest footballing star.

The Belgian team is then announced and all the goodwill is cancelled. The Japanese crowd boos every Belgian name. The goodwill and internationalisation shown outside has disappeared, replaced with a fervent, albeit footballing, nationalism.

Japan must win!

The photographers are led down the sides of the pitch to the tunnel. When the volunteers holding the ropes move away and they are free to take their own positions, bedlam ensues. The Japanese photographers in the group, maniacally wide-eyed, sprint, push and frantically shove without a thought for anyone save themselves in an effort to find the best position. Looking somewhat like elderly ladies bursting through the doors of a church hall for a Saturday morning jumble sale, they leave their foreign colleagues flat-footed and bemused.

'Jesus! I've never seen anything like that before!'

The teams come out from the tunnel to the now familiar 'Anthem' by Vangelis and an ecstatic greeting from the crowd.

Philippe Troussier leads out his troops, his translator never more than a few feet away. The noise from the crowd is such that I can hardly hear the photographer next to me when he shouts something to the teams.

The teams line up on the field for the national anthems.

The Belgian national anthem is sung to virtual silence.

'Kimigayo', the Japanese national anthem, has never sounded so moving. Not usually sung by the young, who make up a large percentage of a football crowd, the song, a funereal dirge inspired by an Englishman, is belted out from all sections of the stadium while everyone holds aloft a small Hinomaru. All sides of the stadium are red and white, each individual flag too small to make a big impression, the overall effect is one of thousands of red dots like pimples on a background of white.

Four jets from the Air Self-Defense Force fly overhead, screaming their message of good wishes to the crowd in a well-timed manoeuvre, leaving behind trails of white smoke, startling the crowd.

The national anthem over, the crowd take up a more familiar, more rousing one.

'Ooooooh, oh, oh-oh-oh, oooh, ooooh, oh-oh!'

And the chant followed by three sharp rasps of clapping

'Ni–ppon!' Cha-cha-cha!

'Ni–ppon!' Cha-cha-cha!

'Ni–ppon!' Cha-cha-cha!

With the flags, the anthem, the frenzy of noise in the crowd and the fly-past, Belgium must never have seemed so far away. If ever there was a home fixture, this is it. Expectations are high. No host nation has ever lost its opening game and that is not the sort of sensation the crowd have in mind.

The Japanese team put their arms around each other's shoulders, form a ring and bend down to listen to a word of encouragement from their captain.

William Mattus, the Costa Rican referee, puts his whistle to his lips and blows. The World Cup has started for Japan and is greeted with yet another loud cheer.

The chants, drumming and whistles continue, drowned by yells every time Japan get the ball or boos when Belgium get a free-kick, corner or pass back to their keeper.

The Japanese fight hard for the ball every time they lose it and though

Belgium have more of the opening couple of minutes, suddenly Nakata Hidetoshi collects the ball on the edge of his own box and advances, accompanied by excited roars, into the Belgian half.

Though Japan make occasional forays forward, playing a skillful short-passing game, they never really threaten.

If the crowd go quiet for a moment, a voice screams through a megaphone and they join in the chorus.

'Ni–*pp*on! Ni–*pp*on! Ni–*pp*on!'

Belgium make the most of their physical advantages and when Ichikawa Daisuke breaks down the right, he is brought down by Yves Vanderhaege, who gets a yellow card.

Although the Japanese certainly don't shirk the challenges, Belgium create the better opportunities, Gurt Verheyen heading wide after 22 minutes.

Suzuki Takayuki bursts into the Belgian box, but runs out of space.

Niggling challenges start to fly in the middle of the pitch where the game becomes bogged down. Narazaki Seigo saves from Marc Wilmots, who is unmarked in the box and Belgium dominate.

Toda Kazayuki, self-confessed Japanese hard man, gets a yellow card for a two-footed flying challenge. Japan seem to have lost their way a little until the 35th minute, when Nakata volleys over from 20 yards. While the Japanese defence looks for offside at the other end, the ball breaks to Wilmots whose shot is blocked, then falls to Bart Goor, who shoots wide.

Just before the end of a flat first half, Nakata turns a defender and crosses well for Yanagisawa, who can't quite connect with his head.

Back in Osaka, Takeuchi is watching the game with 10,000 people in Osaka Dome, home to the Kintetsu Buffaloes baseball team. The three huge screens on the baseball pitch have been provided by the Osaka municipal government and admission is free. Takeuchi, though, isn't too impressed.

'It's a bit like being in a stadium, but a bit stupid.'

I'd much rather listen to Takeuchi's mild complaints than the half-time banter between the photographers. Discussing the story about the Spanish team that have saved a dog from a restaurant in Korea, they wonder about dog meat as food.

'It'd depend on the dog. If you weren't hungry you could have Pekinese and chips, or if you were starving you could have Labrador and chips.'

I'm grateful to be distracted by an email on my phone from Kumai, my wife, who tells me that she hasn't seen me on television yet, but will keep her eyes peeled. '*Gambatte!* – Do your best!'

The second half starts with more fouls, and Inamoto Junichi is booked. The game continues in much the same vein and eventually the Belgian possession tells. A free-kick isn't cleared and is lofted back into the box where Wilmots scores from twelve yards with an overhead kick.

Takeuchi thinks it's all over, as Japan always collapse when they go behind, as everyone knows. In Osaka Dome things are really gloomy, everyone has lost hope. Around me in Saitama, the crowd show their displeasure by throwing paper cups onto the pitch.

Japan keep their heads up and fight for every ball.

Suddenly, a long ball by Ono Shinji from deep inside his own half is lofted forward, catching the Belgian defence in two minds. Suzuki steals through three of them and stretches out a toe as he goes to the ground. He connects with the ball just enough to take it past the advancing keeper. It bounces once and seems to take for ever to come to a stop. But it does, and it's in.

GOOO-AAAA-LLLLLL!!!!!

Pandemonium breaks out in the stands. Almost in disbelief, the screams are raised and people jump up and down, their headgear bouncing with them as they celebrate. Suzuki rushes to his team mates in the technical area, his mouth wide open in wonder.

Flags are hoisted all round the ground. Japan are level.

In Osaka, Takeuchi jumps into the air in disbelief that Suzuki, of all people, has scored.

'Even those of us who went to France, where we lost all the games, have ever experienced anything like this in a World Cup game!'

The atmosphere in the Dome has completely changed and in Saitama, as the game re-starts, the singing reaches new levels.

'Ni–ppon! Ni–ppon! Ni–ppon!'

Every Japan pass is cheered, every Belgium touch booed. Appeals are made for every decision and the anthem without words starts up again.

'Ooooooh, oh, oh-oh-oh, oooh, ooooh, oh-oh!'

Verheyen is booked to a chorus of cheers. Jacky Peeters follows him into the referee's book and Belgium are reeling. Japan push forward at every opportunity.

Ono has a free-kick tapped over the bar and then is replaced as Troussier brings on his 'joker', Alessandro 'Alex' Santos, the naturalised Brazilian-Japanese. Ono looks out of sorts, having had appendicitis several days ago.

Yanagisawa breaks through and is brought down on the edge of the box to screams for a penalty. Troussier goes mad, jumping off the bench and screaming, his interpreter jumping and screaming in unison.

Japan keep up the pressure and Japan keep up the noise.

'Ni–ppon! Ni–ppon! Ni–ppon!'

Belgium give away the ball in midfield and Yanagisawa feeds Inamoto, who skips past Eric van Meir and drives a rocket past Geert de Vlieger from just inside the box.

The crowd explodes in ear-splitting screams, both in the stalls and down on the pitch. I have never heard anything quite like it. This is the World Cup and we are beating Belgium!

Inamoto points his finger in front of him and then at his nose, as the Japanese do when referring to themselves. Is he making a point to Arsene Wenger, his Arsenal manager? Is it a show of self-belief or arrogance? Inamoto says later on television that before the game, he and Miyamoto had agreed that should either of them score, they would join fingers in an E.T.-inspired celebration. Miyamoto isn't on the field and Inamoto has a spare finger he can only point at himself.

In Osaka, Takeuchi is out of his seat again, overjoyed that Inamoto has put them ahead, the first time this has ever happened in a World Cup game. As usual though, he has some doubts.

'Inamoto left his position and went forward, so Toda's covering was really good. Inamoto always does this, but he doesn't usually score, he just hits them over the bar. I hope we don't let one in when he goes walkabout again.'

Inamoto squirms away from the mob that has jumped on him, swivels and punches the air. Troussier jumps up, the crowd jumps up and I jump off my seat.

'Yes!'

I feel part of this more than I did when Sol Campbell scored two days ago. Maybe it's the atmosphere in the crowd, maybe it's because I'm only yards away from the goal, maybe it's the players, who are running themselves into the ground in a way that I've never seen England do, but I feel very much a part of this.

'Ooooooh, oh, oh-oh-oh, oooh, ooooh, oh-oh!'

Japan keep pressing and Morishima Hiroaki, on for Suzuki, goes close.

Miyamoto Tsuneyasu comes on for Morioka Ryuzo, debuting the 'Batman' face mask.

Belgium go forward and Narazaki collects.

The noise is still deafening as Belgium go forward and Narazaki punches when he could have collected. From the corner, Japan look panicky at the back and when they clear, it is picked up by Belgium. A ball looped over the top of the defence catches them square, arms raised looking for offside, and Peter van Der Heyden gets clear and lobs the keeper. It is a bad goal to concede and the stadium is suddenly very quiet.

In Osaka, Takeuchi is moaning again.

'We play the offside trap too much, we just raise our hands and look for the decision. Instead of doing that they should be using that hand to stop the ball or the player. It would be better to get a yellow card than concede a goal. They should concentrate more. Idiots!'

The crowd encourage their team and Japan have a couple more reasonable chances and continue to take the game to Belgium, who pick up two more yellow cards keeping them at bay.

Five minutes before the end, Inamoto, after good passing with Nakata Hidetoshi, wriggles around three defenders to put the ball in the net. Pandemonium breaks out again in the stadium, but Inamoto stands up to see a foul has been given.

The crowd is incredulous. Things are being thrown onto the pitch and the referee is being sworn at.

'Are you blind? That was a goal! What are you doing?'

In the last minute, the referee makes amends by turning down a good Belgian appeal for a penalty and the game ends 2–2.

The celebrations are like Japan had won. This is their first point in the World Cup, less than ten years after their professional league started.

Takeuchi says that he didn't see Inamoto's foul, but later, when he sees it on television, he agrees with the referee's decision.

'At least we drew. Most people in the dome thought we were going to win, they couldn't believe we drew. But I was really happy, I thought we could definitely qualify after that. Me and the people with me were the only ones happy with a draw, no one else could believe we didn't win. Things are going according to the "lose one, win one, draw one" plan for qualification. Draw with Belgium, lose to Russia, beat Tunisia and we're in. Before it started, I thought Belgium were stronger than Russia so I am really, really happy. Maybe we can beat Russia.'

Outside Saitama Stadium, there is a lot more internationalisation going on. Aping the adverts that have been on television for weeks and that are shown in the stadium, fans are swapping shirts. Men with men and women with men. The Belgian shirt has two layers, which makes it difficult to get on and off easily. One Japan fan puts his new acquisition on, only to realise it's inside out.

Two beautiful, young Belgian women have a queue of people waiting to have their photo taken with them. They are lapping up the attention and put their arms round the boys that are brave enough to go near. The boys walk away.

'*Mecha ureshii* – I'm really happy!'

It is that sort of night. The sort of night that happens only once.

Two costumed samurai are also happy.

'We were a bit unlucky, but I think we can go through. Where is the ref from?'

'They played their hearts out for us and I'm really proud of them.'

One man wears a giant football suit, his friend a slightly smaller one on his head. They smile.

'Bring on Russia!'

Two high school girls, still wearing their school skirts, but having changed into Japan shirts, say they are happy with the draw, but sad as they didn't get to see their favourite player, Nakayama Gon.

'He's a bit old, but he really gives it his all. We love Gon.'

They wave a Hinomaru flag with his name on it.

Two men in blue body tights start walking back to the station with a young fan with a painted white face and a red foam ball on his nose.

The lines move slowly to the station. Nobody sings. Everybody is very patient, very orderly. Walking across the fields, police stand with megaphones asking people to watch their step, as it is dangerous. It isn't – I couldn't think of anywhere safer to be.

In the station, it's hot and sticky and the same pushing that is evident on any early morning commuter's platform is here. Nobody apologises. People cram onto trains, discussing the possiblilties.

'If we beat Russia, we're through.'

'Not if they beat Belgium by more than we beat them and draw with Tunisia and Tunisia beat us...I think.'

Two girls start talking to me in English.

'Where are you from?'

'England.'

One of them has a sweatband on either wrist, one in Argentina colours, the other Germany.

'Why don't England use the Union Jack?'

'That's the British flag, and lots of people don't like it, especially the Scots and the Irish.'

'Why? Because the English conquered them, then we put all the flags together, that's why it's called the Union flag.'

'So England is different to Scotland?'

'They're different countries.'

'Eh?'

I explain the differences between Britain, the UK and all the home countries. It takes some time and I'm not sure they understand why the Scots, Welsh and Irish would cheer for whoever played against England, or why some English might cheer for Scotland and Wales but everyone would probably cheer for the Irish. Nationalism, real or adopted, is a tricky thing to work out, unless you have a good reason.

'Why do you have Argentina and German sweatbands?'

'I like Batigol, he's really cool, and the Germans are really big and strong.'

At my stop, I get off the train and buy some beers and watch the highlights of the match. I see myself on television, my small digital camera amongst the huge lenses.

The Road to Yokohama   Match 1   May 31 to June 5

Group A

	P	W	D	L	F	A	GD	Pts
Denmark	1	1	0	0	2	1	1	3
Senegal	1	1	0	0	1	0	1	3
Uruguay	1	0	0	1	1	2	-1	0
France	1	0	0	1	0	1	-1	0

May 31 France 0 1 Senegal
Seoul
June 1 Uruguay 1 2 Denmark
Ulsan

Group B

	P	W	D	L	F	A	GD	Pts
Spain	1	1	0	0	3	1	2	3
Paraguay	1	0	1	0	2	2	0	1
S. Africa	1	0	1	0	2	2	0	1
Slovenia	1	0	0	1	1	3	-2	0

June 2 Paraguay 2 2 S. Africa
Busan
June 2 Spain 3 1 Slovenia
Gwangju

Group C

	P	W	D	L	F	A	GD	Pts
Costa Rica	1	1	0	0	2	0	2	3
Brazil	1	1	0	0	2	1	1	3
Turkey	1	0	0	1	1	2	-1	0
China	1	0	0	1	0	2	-2	0

June 3 Brazil 2 1 Turkey
Ulsan
June 4 China 0 2 Costa Rica
Gwangju

Group D

	P	W	D	L	F	A	GD	Pts
S. Korea	1	1	0	0	2	0	2	3
USA	1	1	0	0	3	2	1	3
Portugal	1	0	0	1	2	3	-1	0
Poland	1	0	0	1	0	2	-2	0

June 4 South Korea 2 0 Poland
Busan
June 5 USA 3 2 Portugal
Suwon

Group E

	P	W	D	L	F	A	GD	Pts
Germany	1	1	0	0	8	0	8	3
Cameroon	1	0	1	0	1	1	0	1
Ireland	1	0	1	0	1	1	0	1
Saudi Arabia	1	0	0	1	0	8	-8	0

June 1 Ireland 1 1 Cameroon
Niigata
June 1 Germany 8 0 Saudi Arabia
Sapporo

Group F

	P	W	D	L	F	A	GD	Pts
Argentina	1	1	0	0	1	0	1	3
England	1	0	1	0	1	1	0	1
Sweden	1	0	1	0	1	1	0	1
Nigeria	1	0	0	1	0	1	-1	0

June 2 England 1 1 Sweden
Saitama
June 2 Argentina 1 0 Nigeria
Ibaraki

Group G

June 3 Croatia 0 1 Mexico
Niigata
June 3 Italy 2 0 Ecuador
Sapporo

	P	W	D	L	F	A	GD	Pts
Italy	1	1	0	0	2	0	2	3
Mexico	1	1	0	0	1	0	1	3
Croatia	1	0	0	1	0	1	-2	0
Ecuador	1	0	0	1	0	2	-2	0

Group H

June 4 Japan 2 2 Belgium
Saitama
June 5 Russia 2 0 Tunisia
Kobe

	P	W	D	L	F	A	GD	Pts
Russia	1	1	0	0	2	0	2	3
Belgium	1	0	1	0	2	2	0	1
Japan	1	0	1	0	2	2	0	1
Tunisia	1	0	0	1	0	2	-2	0

we are nippon

7

I'm Not a Hooligan

After the draw for the World Cup was made, in December 2001, the build up to the Japanese half of the tournament concentrated on the teams that would be coming. Those teams included England and, everyone expected, the hooligans that they would be bringing with them.

Television documentaries and news programmes showed footage of hooligans running amok in towns all over Europe. The Japanese television audience was treated to highlights of English hooligans' career of violence in Marseille, France 1998, Charleroi, Belgium 2000 and even Heysel Stadium, Belgium again, in 1995. It didn't take long for the opinion to be formed that Japan was in grave danger of being attacked by barbarians from England. Not all the footage of hooligans shown was of the English, but everyone assumed that it was. No mention was made of the problems in Argentinian or Italian football. Hooliganism was again portrayed as the English Disease.

It was taken as a given that there would be trouble. As the media whipped the country into a paranoid frenzy, the nation's police forces, particularly those in Saitama, Sapporo and Osaka, where England would play their three group games, began preparations.

In Sapporo, 7,000 extra police were drafted in from other parts of the country, almost one extra officer for every England supporter expected. The expanded force invested in some new hardware.

A television program delighted in displaying the strength of the new defensive shields that had been developed to deal with the *furigan,*as the word is rendered in the local parlance. A camera behind a shield seemed to wince as a sledgehammer was brought upon the shield at full force. The shield stayed intact.

Drawing on an anti-hooligan budget equivalent to £22.8 million, police armed themselves with leg braces and a kind of wire noose mounted on a long pole, designed to help them cope with the foreign hooligans who were expected to be much larger then them. The braces could be manipulated in such a way as to bring down an attacker from a safe distance.

At the unveiling of the medieval-looking contraption, a helpful police spokesman explained the thinking behind the device.

'The best way to defeat taller opponents would be to trip them up and then subdue them on the ground.'

Another such device to get the opponent down for subduing was the net gun, a Spiderman-like contraption that shoots heavy nets over hooligans to entrap them. The device was tested on actors posing as hooligans – English hooligans, wearing England strips and waving England flags – successfully ensnaring them from a distance of 16 feet.

More dress-rehearsals were held at stadiums where mock riots, again featuring actors in England shirts, were conducted to give the police a little target practice.

In Osaka, the stones on the railway lines that run near Nagai Stadium, where England would play Nigeria, were glued down lest they be hurled anywhere. Leaflets were distributed to houses as far as five miles away from the stadium, telling residents to look out for hooligans, to pull down any shutters they had and not to leave things such as bicycles and pot plants outside.

Police forces bought huge anti-riot vehicles with large, programmable digital signs that displayed slogans like, 'We are the police. Calm down.'

Special police units visited England and videoed crowds at games and consulted with their English colleagues.

A mild form of hysteria gripped the nation and several people interviewed on television or in the papers said they would either leave the country or escape to relatives' houses in the countryside, far away from the danger.

In Osaka, shopkeepers near the stadium took out insurance for ¥5,000 (£27.50) each, covering them for approximately ¥10 million (£55,000) worth of damage during the World Cup. Elementary and junior high schools were to close on match days to protect pupils from any violence. Many parents were reported as saying they would simply keep their children, their dogs and belongings locked firmly indoors.

In Miyagi, a local politician warned of foreigners selling cocaine and heroin and burning parked cars, while Konno Takayoshi, of the ruling Liberal Democratic Party, the party of Prime Minister Koizumi Junichiro, said that the country should, 'also brace against unwanted babies being conceived by foreigners who rape our women. We must prepare for the worst.'

In response, the British Embassy and the Osaka Supporters Club, led by Takeuchi, tried to calm nerves. A national newspaper printed the flag of St. George with the message, 'Against Violence!' Takeuchi was livid.

'Why pick on the English? I've seen fights at J.League games – fistfights, stone-throwing and burning.'

In an effort to show people that not all fans are hooligans and that just because someone is shouting and singing, it doesn't mean they are violent, OSC printed T-shirts with the slogan 'I'm not a hooligan', in English and Japanese, and started wearing them at World Cup-related events, J.League games and international friendlies.

The British Embassy printed leaflets explaining the appearance, attitudes and actions of the visitors soon to arrive in their thousands. Japanese might, the leaflet explained, be scared by the fans' big bodies, but shouldn't be put off by the large numbers of fans, who would have saved money for months to make this trip to Japan, most of them for the first time.

The fans shouldn't be viewed as a threat, the leaflet went on, rather, if people learned a few simple words and phrases such as 'Welcome!', 'Can I help you?' and 'England are a great team!', they would soon make new friends. Their new friends, of course, would have beer-bellies and possibly tattoos and accents that made them difficult to understand. The leaflet, therefore, advised that people should carry dictionaries and pieces of paper to aid communication.

The leaflet said that fans gather in parks and pubs before games, displaying their flags and singing songs, displaying their pride in their country.

A once-in-a-lifetime event, this international festival, the leaflet continued, would be a chance for international eating, singing, dancing and drinking.

Also organized were public relations events in Osaka and Sapporo to help calm the locals' nerves. The English Football Supporters Association was represented by Kevin Miles, manager of the fans' embassies. An ex-television reporter acting as MC went on at length about the war-like English character and that they were undefeated in any war since 1066. A panelist agreed, adding that if there were any trouble, the Japanese police would be in for a real hiding.

With things not quite proceeding as planned, an embassy staff member discretely asked the panel to move on and Miles added that, although he had a skinhead, was big, fat and ugly, he wasn't a hooligan and nor were 99% of fans that looked just like him.

Miles' remarks went down well, one man in the audience commenting that perhaps Japanese people should try to be a bit more understanding of others and should welcome the English.

There was a slight improvement in awareness. Mabuchi Ryogo, a sociologist at Nara University, added to the debate by pointing out that the crime rate among foreigners living in Japan is actually much lower than among Japanese, but that, 'many Japanese still have a biased image.'

In the days leading up to the final, several Britons were denied entry to the country. Prince Takamado expressed worries that the image of armed riot police, ready to do battle with hooligans, would create an environment where trouble was more likely to occur.

Certainly, the attitude of the police would be a deciding factor if there were any trouble. When an official at Osaka City Hall was asked if he was worried about the police over-reacting and actually causing trouble rather than preventing it, he replied that, far from being worried about the police being too strict, he was worried about them not being strict enough.

The prince more sensibly suggested that if people were welcomed as guests, they would, in all likeliness, not cause trouble, and that people should not assume all fans were hooligans. The worst thing that could happen, he thought, was that Japanese people would ignore all foreigners because of misunderstanding and fear and that people would leave the country thinking that the Japanese were cold-hearted.

Takamodo's message, though a very reasonable one, did not seem to be getting through. Ten days before the tournament began, two Argentina fans wearing their country's colours and carrying rucksacks, walked down a street in Hirono, Fukushima, where the Argentina team were based. They were detained by a force of eight riot police and four patrol cars. Numerous residents had called police and said that the town was swarming with hooligans. After checking the fans' passports and making sure that they had accommodation, they were released by police, their only crime being to walk through a maelstrom of paranoia.

Before the tournament kicked-off, there seemed to be a delicate balance between a willingness to welcome supporters with open arms, or handle them with extreme care. Whichever attitude prevailed would likely dictate the mood of the World Cup.

8

Sapporo Clasico – England vs. Argentina

Argentinian football owes everything it has to England. The English in Argentina started the game there, giving the clubs they formed English names that are still familiar today – Boca Juniors, Racing Club, River Plate and Newell's Old Boys.

The game was played by English and Italians working on the railways that were built in the latter half of the 19th century. The first recorded game, noted in the *Standard*, was played at Buenos Aires Cricket Club on June 20, 1867, between the White Caps and the Red Caps, each of which only had eight players, all British.

The story goes that a local boy asked his father who the strange people were that were chasing a ball around a field. They are Ingleses, his father told him. 'Ingleses locos.' Crazy Englishmen. The crazy Englishmen in white beat the crazy Englishmen in red 4-0.

Watson Hutton, an English schoolteacher and the headmaster of St. Andrew's School in Buenos Aires, started the first Argentine football league, The Argentine Association Football League, in 1891. All the teams in the league, Buenos Aires FC, Belgrano Football Club, Buenos Aires al Rosario Railway, Saint Andrew's and the first-ever champions, Old Caledonians, were again made up of British players. One Charles Moffat of the Old Caledonians scored a hat-trick in the play-off against Saint Andrew's to win the championship.

The league was disbanded after that season and became The Argentine Association Football League in 1893, only to be re-named The Argentine Association Football League again in 1903.

The winning club of the 1911 Argentine Football Association, Porteño, included names such as the Italian Cuchi, Berisso, Bacigaluppi and Piaggio, and the Spanish Márquez. The game was losing its English domination and the number of Italian names hints at an Argentinian paradox.

Although a Spanish-speaking nation, a larger percentage of the surnames in Argentina are of Italian origin than Spanish, and though this population didn't manage to replace the language it found when it arrived, the Spanish spoken in Argentina has a strong Italian accent. The English, with their clubs for crazy games and afternoon teas in hotels, also left an influence so strong that today it is said an Argentinian speaks Spanish like an Italian and thinks he's an Englishman.

Afternoon tea, 'El five o'clock tea', is taken in more homes in Buenos Aires than in London. When the rich send their children to school, it is to the English-style schools in the suburbs that they go – the aforementioned St. Andrew's, Northlands and Saint Hilda's. There is an admiration for things English, explained by the saying, 'When it rains in London, the umbrellas come out in Buenos Aires.' English football has also left its mark on the language, whereas in Spain they talk of *delantero*, *saque de esquina* and *extremo*, in Argentina, they use the English terms forward, corner and wing.

Next to the admiration, there is also a festering resentment.

Initially excluded from the game that they came to love by the English who brought it to them, the Argentinians feel a resentment toward the English like a schoolboy would to his master, a master they see as having a misplaced sense of superiority.

Roberto Perfumo, journalist, author and one-time Argentinian captain, said that, for them, beating England in the famous game in Mexico in 1986 was more important than winning the final itself. He goes on to speak of an Oedipus complex.

The Falklands War had ended only four years earlier, with many Argentinians feeling intense anger at what they saw as a first-world power taking on a third-world nation.

The football fixture, though, has a history longer than David Beckham and Diego Simeone in France or Maradona and the 'Hand of God' in 1986. In Argentina, they say it's like a derby match, a clasico – a classic.

Any Englishman of a certain age will remember that in 1966, when captain Antonio Rattin was sent off at Wembley against England, he refused to leave the pitch for a full ten minutes. At the end of the game Alf Ramsey went onto the pitch to stop George Cohen swapping shirts with Perfumo. Ramsey later famously labelled the Argentinians as 'animals', something that has never been forgotten or forgiven. The Argentinians responded to this insult by saying that an English FA official had kicked a pregnant Argentinian woman in the stomach.

In 1977, during another match, this time at the Boca Juniors' stadium in Buenos Aires, Trevor Cherry was punched by Bertoni, losing two of his teeth. Bertoni's hand still apparently bears the scars.

In 1986 came the Hand of God, which scarred all of England and then Simeone and Beckham in France 98. When Aldo Duscher, once of Newell's Old Boys, then of Deportivo La Coruña, made a two-foot lunge at David Beckham, breaking his metatarsal and, everyone thought at the time, knocking him out of the 2002 World Cup, the conspiracy theories ran rampant in England. Argentina's daily sports paper, *Olé*, however, simply ran the headline – 'Duscher – national hero.'

Added to all of this is the fact that the fans of both countries' teams have unparalleled reputations for football-related violence. The Argentinians have a particularly virulent strain of the English Disease and in the last ten years, around 50 people have been killed at Argentine football games. In the 2001-2002 season, five people were killed and there were numerous knife and shotgun assaults.

The clash in Sapporo, in the 20th anniversary year of the Falklands War, was expected to be a fierce encounter, both on and off the field.

Hokkaido has a somewhat troubled relationship with the outside world and at times with the rest of Japan. On Hokkaido, the people of Honshu are still sometimes referred to as *naijin*, meaning inside people or mainlanders. They are traditionally seen as an untrustworthy, undesirable and loathsome lot to the people of Hokkaido, as the English are to the Scots. In 2000, the brother of an acquaintance, a university student in Sapporo, was refused permission to marry his girlfriend, a local, whose parents said he wasn't suitable as he was *naijin*.

To the north of Hokkaido lie the Kuril Islands. These islands have been the subject of a territorial dispute since the end of WWII when they were grabbed by the Russians in the final days of conflict. There are disputes over fishing rights and many Russian vessels use the northern waters around Hokkaido, necessitating berths in local ports.

After trouble with drunken Russian sailors in the town of Otaru, many Japanese bath houses and hot-springs banned foreigners from their premises. A local American-born university lecturer, who had become a naturalised Japanese national, went to one of the hot-springs and was denied entry under the 'no-foreigners' rule. When he pointed out that he was actually Japanese, he was barred entry because he 'looked foreign to Japanese eyes.'

For the match between Argentina and England on June 6 in Sapporo, a lot more foreigners would be seen.

On June 5, I rise at 6.15 a.m., after having gone to bed just three hours earlier. I take the monorail to Tokyo's Haneda Airport and after a short flight, during which we are served coffee and reminded that Japan Airlines (JAL) is not serving alcohol on its domestic flights for the duration of the tournament. Those that are truly bothered by this at such an un-godly hour, and there are some, have planned ahead and bought cans of beer from the convenience store in the airport. If someone is going to get drunk and fly into air rage, at least JAL won't get the blame.

When we arrive at Sapporo – World Cup motto: 'Cosmopolitan city with international events; Proof of the real value' – coming through the gates into the main airport building, several camera crews from the TV news stations are waiting, as are significant numbers of the local constabulary. One camera crew point their camera at me. I lift my hand to obscure the lens and the cameraman immediately drops his camera to the ground and looks suitably admonished. He is obviously not a FIFA-accredited man.

I have arrived without anywhere to stay, so stroll over to the hotel information desk and ask about a business hotel for two nights.

Contrary to popular belief, hotels in Japan can be very cheap. There are dozens of 'business hotels' near the main station in any city. These hotels are basic and cater, as the name suggests, mainly to business people working away from home. The rooms provide a bed and an *en suite* bathroom, usually a 'unit bathroom' where the entire thing is made from one piece of moulded plastic and is so small that taking a shower invariably means the toilet paper gets saturated. There is also a phone line, optional breakfast and, of course, a television with a pay-per-view porn channel. The kind of pornography on offer is the kind where seemingly stupid, very young-looking girls pander, in high-pitched voices, to their older lovers' whims. The kind of person Japan expects to be staying near a train station for the purpose of doing business is obviously male, middle-aged, working for a company on a tight budget, uncomfortable with women his own age and in possession of extremely poor taste and a very fragile ego.

The other option for the budget-constrained businessman, or salaryman, is the famed capsule hotel. More likely to be used by salarymen that have had far too much to drink and have missed the last train home, the capsule hotel is even smaller than a business hotel. The room, or capsule, is not much bigger than a plastic coffin, and row upon row of these are stacked on top of one another and entered by ladders as you would a set of multi-tiered bunk-beds. The hotels have a communal bathing area and inside the capsule is a place to hang your suit, a clock and a TV with pay-per-view pornography.

Never having stayed in a capsule hotel, I was keen to sample the delights of Safro Spa in the city centre. A well-known hotel, Safro Spa also features a pool and bath-house complex, a beauty salon, massage room, boutique, restaurant and separate women's and men's capsule accommodation. All this is advertised on their website, www.safro.org, where, in the true spirit of internationalisation, the salient points are highlighted in English, adding that killer cosmopolitan touch. The browser is encouraged to enjoy Safro 'Amusement' which 'gives peple [sic] smaile [sic], laugh, pleasure or entertainment.' A place where people can enjoy food and 'flesh.' Not a sample of the cuisine on offer nor an invitation to sin with girls with high-pitched voices, but a misspelling of the word 'fresh', its intended use here being a verb, meaning to refresh oneself and relax.

All of these are tempting attractions and, still in the cosmopolitan English language, we are promised 'rest, and amusement, or an activity' and invited to choose from a series of buttons.

'Eat! Beauty! Relax! Reserve!'

All of this for only ¥3,500 (around £19) a night. It was too good to resist.

As I had been travelling to and from Ibaraki with a hoard of happily drunk Irishmen, I'd seen all this on the Internet in the media centre at the

Ibaraki Prefectural Stadium and had then asked Kumai to make a reservation for me. The conversation she had went like this.

'I'd like to make a reservation for June the 6th and 7th, are there any rooms available?'

'Yes there are, how many people?'

'Just one.'

'Could I have the name and telephone number, please?'

'Simo...'

'Ah! No foreigners here.'

'What? But you said there were rooms available, didn't you?'

'Yes, there are, but not for foreign customers.'

'Why?'

'Because they are foreign.'

'That's the only reason?'

'Yes.'

In Sapporo, tired and hung-over, without a bed for the next two nights, I approach the reservation desk at the airport in some trepidation, a little weary of the spirit of internationalisation and friendliness the rest of the country and its visitors seem to be caught up in.

'*Haro.*' I am greeted in English.

'*Haro,*' I reply in the same, then add, in Japanese, 'Are there any business hotels vacant for tonight and tomorrow?'

'Mmmh, let me see, that might be a little difficult.'

This phrase, 'a little difficult', is often heard and though seemingly encouraging, in that the intended offer of service may be a little difficult to provide but you are assured the best efforts will be made. Its actual intended meaning is more often 'absolutely not', though not many people, the bad-mannered staff at the Safro excluded, would actually come out and say so to your face.

'I'll have a look, but I think everywhere is fully-booked.'

The young woman behind the counter, decked out in her standard-issue airport uniform of cheap, bright blue polyester, satin tie, peaked cap and enough gold braid to signify a high-rank in an imaginary navy, picks up a book that, in Japanese, says on the front, 'Hotels That Will Accept Foreigners'.

'Mmmh. It's a bit difficult, you see, all of these are full. I'll have a look on the computer.'

There is another book on the desk, this one says, 'Hotels That Won't Accept Foreigners'. The Safro is not alone in its guest policy and the poor girl in the bright mixed fibres and natty cap has to do the dirty work.

'Mmmh, there's only one room. It doesn't have a window and I think it's only free tonight, there's nothing for tomorrow. I'll have to check again in a moment.'

Her assistant has taken a telephone call, opened the other book and made a reservation on the computer which she is now using, having placed the book back down on the desk.

'What about the hotels in the other book, are any of those available?'

'Uhm, they don't speak English at those hotels, so it would be a little difficult for you to make a reservation there.'

'Well, that's fine, because I can speak Japanese, so I wouldn't have any problems.'

'Of course you can speak Japanese, but as they don't speak English, it might be a little difficult. Just a moment please.'

Static electricity sparks as the woman's skirt brushes along the nylon cloth of the computer chair.

'Ah! The room is free for two nights, but it doesn't have a window. What shall we do?'

'How much is it?'

'¥4,500 a night.'

'We'll take it.'

I take the train into the city centre, after suffering more mangled English mumbled back to me at the FIFA information desk when I ask where the subway entrance is. The hotel is just across the road from the station.

On the television in my windowless room, the news reports that foreigners are arriving at the airport in droves. I rather hope to see myself hiding my face somewhat melodramatically with my hand, but the cameraman must have done as my gesture suggested. The report also shows the shutters going up on a high percentage of the bars and restaurants in the city, saying that many would stay closed, giving their staff a paid night off and apologising to their regulars. The teams had arrived to the usual fanfare and much screaming at Beckham, though his popularity, unchallenged against Sweden, has a minor rival in the number of girls screaming for Gabriel 'Batigol' Batistuta.

The news also shows that the fans are gathering in Oyogi Park, which runs through the centre of the city, east to west.

Although Sapporo is a large city and home to 1.8 million people, it has an easily navigable centre. Laid out sensibly on a grid system, addresses are given as their block number and a compass reference, hence, the first bar I try to find to watch the France vs. Uruguay game, Bar Jersey, is at West 6, South 3.

Bar Jersey, being a sports bar well-advertised on English-language World Cup websites, is packed. The customers are spilling down the stairs, the top of which reek of sweat and lager. Cockney-, Brummie- and Scouse-accented expletives are being directed at the French. The game has just started. I decide on my second choice, Beer Inn Mugishutei at South 9, West 5, run by an American who brews his own beer, Ezo, the old name for Hokkaido.

Hurrying along, I pick up three lost Englishmen, who are standing in the middle of the street. One of them, wearing a red England away shirt, stretched tightly over his enormous beer-belly, his white face pink from too much sun, is asking a taxi driver where they can watch the football.

'Excuse me, where can we watch the football?'

'*Aimu so-ree, ai donto speeku Eengureeshu.*'

The taxi driver had obviously been studying.

'You know, football.' The beer-bellied Englishman adds cheerily as he kicks the air to demonstrate his country's national sport, as unconvincingly as England had in the second half against Sweden.

The taxi driver smiles and swats his hand to and fro in front of his face, as if batting away some unwelcome smell or annoying insect, indicating he doesn't understand.

The Englishman is not put off.

'You know, television.' He draws an imaginary television in the air by joining his index fingers together in front of his face and making an imaginary box, as if introducing a television program in a badly-contested game of charades, repeating, 'Television, television.'

The taxi driver looks on, puzzled in the extreme, struggling manfully to prevent his face giving away his thoughts.

'Who is this strange, fat, white man, and what on earth is he gesturing about?'

'I know a bar that's showing the game if you'd like to join me,' I say, without breaking stride.

'Great, hang on a second.'

All three immediately fall in, one turning and directing a 'thank you!' to the taxi driver as they do so.

'*Sank-yoo.*'

We find Mugishutei and are served pints of a lethal brew. As we watch the game, my new friends show a dislike for the French that the receptionist at Safro Spa would be proud of.

'I hate the French, me.'

'Why's that?'

'Two reasons: first, they're arrogant. Second, they're French.'

The universal reason of international football supporters and hotel workers. Do Frenchmen in London get denied hotel rooms, I wonder, do the French in Senegal or the Senegalese in Paris? Can the love of your own country only be suitably expressed by the disdain of another? At least he gave one more reason than the receptionist at Safro.

Mugishutei is selling *World Geppu* (burp) T-shirts featuring a burping football on the front and the translation of the word 'burp' into the languages of the nations competing in the World Cup on the back. This brought a lawsuit from FIFA, who complained the bar was hijacking their event. Mugishutei won.

The next day, the hangover from the Ezo beer not quite worn off, I make my way to Oyogi Park, realising on the way that my mobile phone's

battery has gone flat. This being a country where phone-jacking is un-
heard of and civility runs deep, I ask in a rival mobile phone supplier's
shop where I might find a Tu-ka Station, the name given to the shops run
by the company I rent my phone from, so that I might get a re-charge. I am
politely directed to the nearest shop and ushered on my way with a bow.

The Tu-ka Station is a few blocks down and when I get there I ask the
receptionist how long it will take to re-charge my phone. About 40 minutes, she replies, giving me enough time to then check my email on the
high-speed internet terminals provided free of charge in the shop and get
some breakfast away from the hordes flocking into McDonald's and
Starbucks. In the small café, the television is showing a documentary shot
the previous night.

A camera crew from a local Sapporo TV station accompanied a police
patrol car around the city. Lots of drunk England and Argentina supporters are seen, singing and dancing in the streets. A call comes over the radio
and the patrol car rushes off to where seven or eight policemen are grap-
pling with an England fan who is being arrested. Here is a hooligan being
detained, the TV station says, and look how big he is, it needs that many
officers to restrain him.

It later turns out that the man was arrested for taking someone's hat
from his head, after which they got into an argument.

For the rest of the evening, the police are called to two more incidents,
one at an *izakaya*, another at a bar. As the reporter says, though, these are
not hooligans, they are just young Japanese people who have had too much
to drink, causing them to fight.

When I get back to the Tu-ka Station, sweating after only a short walk,
a middle-aged English couple are marvelling at the phones on the rack
outside. They are about to try to buy one before I tell them that the phones
will only work in Japan. The market for mobiles in Japan is so big that,
although the phones and the technology they use would be an instant hit
abroad, Japanese companies don't even bother to try to supply the international market as they can't keep up with the domestic one. NTT DoCoMo
has recently licensed the technology to Europe, though for now, while the
English have to content themselves with ringtones any self-respecting twelve-
year-old Japanese kid would be too embarrassed to play on a Stylophone,
the locals have animated colour graphics, graphic-enhanced email, a host
of websites, phones equipped with cameras to send photographs, Global
Positioning System-powered maps and ringtones with polyphonic voices
and scores as complicated as an opera.

In Oyogi Park, a large crowd has gathered. The English fans are there,
their tops off, enjoying the sun and cans of lager. The Argentinians are
there, a few with their tops off, a few enjoying the sun and lager. Japanese
English fans are there, their faces painted, wigs on their heads and England
strips with the number seven or ten on their backs. There are Japanese-

Argentina fans, again faces painted, caped in the flag of their temporarily-adopted nation.

There are England fans from Hong Kong, Singapore, Trinidad and Australia; Asian-English fans and black-English fans. The Argentinian fans mingle with the English, singing each other's songs and waving each other's flags. The language spoken by all is English, the international language and the only one the English can speak. The Argentinians here speak it well and seem well-educated. Only the richer fans can afford the trip, one tells me.

The same is true of the English; the majority are a different type of fan than is often associated with England. Not the rioters of Lansdowne Road or Marseille, but the long-haul traveller and ex-pat. Fans have flown in from all over the world, just for this game.

The Argentinian songs are accompanied by drums, dancing and South American rhythms the English just don't seem able to match. Games of five-a-side and keepy-up stretch all over the park. The English are a very poor second in terms of skill and style to their new Argentinian friends, many of whom excel at football and close control, the ball dancing from foot to foot.

If this ability carries over onto the pitch, the police may have something to worry about after the game.

For now, though, all is a perfect model of international friendship and bridge-building. Fans stand on the fences where the park meets the pavement and is intersected by a road. Arm in arm, they sing with each other. Argentina, England, Japan-Argentina, England, Japan-England, Japan.

The Japanese are being taught the words to some songs and in places, a little menace lurks underneath the good humour.

'Give us back the Falklands, you little English whores!'

Across the road in another section of the park.

'No surrender, no surrender, no surrender to the IRA!'

Thankfully, no one seems to understand what the others are singing, least of all the Japanese.

As the numbers standing on the fences increase, the police stand in a row on the road opposite them, watching, more anxious and unsure than menacing. A policeman in the park does his best to protect the flowerbeds that are being trampled underfoot, urging a Japanese youth to be careful, addressing him respectfully with the term used for one's elder brother.

'*Oni-san*, move back please, be careful of the flowers!'

Girls gather on the fringes, watching the commotion, a few are brave enough to offer greetings in broken English. All seem fascinated. An elderly woman, oblivious to all the commotion, sleeps curled up under the umbrella she has put up to protect her from the sun.

Everyone takes everyone else's photo. One family, noticing my press badge, takes my photo, as I 'must be important.'

Everyone wishes everyone else well. The white English skins are burning and the lager is taking its effect. People begin to move to the subway station.

The station is a mass of people. The fans of England and Argentina, though mainly England, move amongst the shoppers and the salarymen, the housewives and the school kids, directed by girls in the blue tracksuit-uniform of the FIFA volunteers, holding signs with arrows pointing to cartoon trains, standing only a few metres from the very obvious entrance to the station concourse.

Signs on the ceiling above the stairs to the concourse welcome the visitors in the languages of the countries competing at Sapporo: Arabic, German, Spanish, English, Italian and Spanish again. Each poster shows a fan of each country's team in team colours and face paint and the occasional silly hat, the *de rigueur* uniform of the modern international football fan.

After buying tickets, as a group descends the escalators to the platform, one England fan begins humming the theme from *The Great Escape*.

'It's not that sort of tunnel!'

Everyone moves on to the train, spirits high, swapping stories of the kindness of the Japanese, the Argentinian history they had just learned in the park from their new Argentinian friends and predicting the score as the train pulls out towards Fukuzumi Station.

Along the route of the ten-minute walk from the station to the dome, the streets are lined with stalls selling food and drink and the usual peddlers of unofficial merchandise. One tells me he has made ¥1 million, about £5,400, selling shirts here and at the Sweden game. Further along are Japanese men standing outside a car showroom, selling tickets. The men sport natty perms and wear matching knitted-cotton trouser and jersey suits, some embroidered with large, colourful pictures of cartoon animals. Comic-looking to the unaware, the men are easily identifiable as *chinpira*, low-ranking *yakuza*.

The tickets are Category Three tickets, with a face value of $60, about £40. The price being asked is ¥100,000, around £540. I ask one man how business is, how many tickets he has sold at that price. He replies with a simple gesture, holding his thumb and forefinger over an inch apart. He tells me that they don't get into fights with foreign touts, just as one walks over and he and his Japanese colleague slap each other on the back firmly and grin, playfully pushing each other away in mock combat.

Internationalisation is proceeding well in the darker business quarters of Sapporo.

A few metres along from the touts, I turn a corner and there is the latest, and surely most memorable, location of the next installment in the series of England-Argentina Clasicos – the Sapporo Dome.

Sapporo Dome was built in 2001 for ¥53.7 billion (approx. £293 million) including the cost of the land it stands on. The dome, construction of which cost around £230 million, less than a third of the £715 million needed to fund the building of the new Wembley Stadium, is home to J.League team Consadole Sapporo and is also used for baseball, conferences, concerts and exhibitions. A futuristic building for most, there are so many futuristic buildings in Japan that the word here is in danger of losing its meaning. The Sapporo Dome is the seventh such structure in the country and looks somewhat like a giant, galvanized computer mouse.

Designed to accommodate both football and baseball, games with completely different fields and sitting arrangements, not to mention the concerts and exhibitions, the Sapporo Dome is multi-purpose and employs a unique floating pitch. When being used for baseball, the soccer pitch sits outside the ground, allowing the grass to grow under the elements and removing the need for anything as antiquated as a retractable roof. When it is to be used for football, the pitcher's mound descends into the floor, the artificial turf of the baseball field is rolled up and removed, the seats next to the 90-metre opening door slide out of the way, the doors open and the football field is moved in. The world's first 'Hovering Soccer Field' weighs 8,300 tons, equivalent to about 30 jumbo jets, and is moved in on a cushion of air, which reduces its weight by 90%, it then moves on 34 wheels at a speed of four metres per minute. The seats that usually surround the baseball diamond rotate into positions alongside the football pitch and, once inside the dome, the pitch and seats rotate 90 degrees together on the air-cushion, the open-close seats slide back round into position and the huge door closes, putting the stadium in 'soccer-mode.' The operation takes around two hours.

The stadium has air-conditioning in summer and heating in winter. As the official literature says, there is no rain or snow here, there are only dreams. There is also an observatory with commanding views of Sapporo, a 230-seat restaurant, a concourse with an 18-metre atrium and a 150-metre-long, glass dome-sheltered 'town' with shops, restaurants and cafés. There are two basement floors, four above ground and two penthouse levels. The Sapporo Dome also has a fan club, whose members get a regular newsletter.

The most amazing thing about the dome, about the whole operation, is that everyone seems to take it in their stride. That this sort of project doesn't really seem to amaze anyone, is itself amazing. Sapporo Dome is to be used for three games during the World Cup.

Inside the dome, taking the stairs to the top floor to go to the media tribune seats, I bump into Terry Butcher, who, in 1986 before the Hand of God game, had explained on television how he would deal with Maradona: 'Kick him.'

When I reminded him of this and what advice he would give to the team these days, he is less bullish.

'They've got so many good players, you deal with one and another one comes at you. I said that at the time for a bit of a laugh, but you can't go round kicking people these days.'

Inside the dome, descending the stairs to my seat, the stadium is almost full, an hour before kick-off. All around, the seats are a sea of red and white, whether they are visiting England fans or the locals, all have come in the team's colours, and England considerably outnumber Argentina. England are again the home team.

Three-quarters of an hour before kick-off, Davids Seaman and James come onto the pitch to loud cheers and the singing, sporadic up until now, goes up a significant level, the extra syllable helping the chant along.

'Engerland, Engerland, Engerland!'

The keepers have to climb the stairs up to the pitch, which sits raised above the ground. The effect is like climbing onto a stage.

The cheering and singing continue, the noise level rising with each new chorus, the Japanese joining in, the extra syllable making the pronunciation easier at the beginning, though some still tended to slip an extra one on the end.

'*Ingarando, Ingarando, Ingarando!*'

The stadium is the busiest yet. Hassled volunteers are harried by late-comers hurrying the wrong way. They are shown to their seats, not noticing the extra numbers of orange-bib-wearing police.

The teams are out and during the roll call, only the England fans can be heard, Beckham and Owen both getting noisy, high-pitched cheers. The flags are out and being passed above the heads of the crowd, the drums accompanying the chants.

'ENGLAND-Du-Du-Du! ENGLAND-Du-Du-Du!'

The Argentinian anthem is booed throughout by the English fans as the Argentinian contingent sing.

Mortals! Hear the sacred cry,
Freedom! Freedom! Freedom!
We salute the great people of Argentina,
And the free peoples of the world reply,
We salute the great people of Argentina!

'God Save the Queen' is then similarly booed by the great people of Argentina, who, their flags hoisted saying the Falklands belong to them, don't appear to want to be long-reigned over. The English fans sing loudly and enthusiastically and again miss their cue, ending up out of sync with the piped music and finishing too early, having to repeat the end of the song. This being an unofficial sort of patriotism, the patriots that sing, 'I'm English till I die', neither know all the words, nor the tune and the timing, to their official national anthem.

The announcer with the Disneyland voice runs through the FIFA-UNICEF nonsense about creating one world for children, the mascots run off the field and the strains of *The Great Escape* can be heard somewhere beneath the feverish exhortations being yelled in English, Spanish and Japanese.

The roar at kick-off is as thunderous as the flashes are blinding and England vs. Argentina, the fifth part of this special World Cup series, is underway.

As the theme from *The Great Escape* continues, six minutes into the game an Argentine defender, coming into possession on the edge of his own box, waltzes easily past three Englishmen like he is playing in Oyogi Park with a can of lager in his hand.

Most of the English crowd don't seem to notice and a chorus rings around the dome, the atmosphere undisturbed by being enclosed by a roof.

'I'm English till I die, I'm English till I die, I know I am, I'm sure I am, I'm English till I die!'

As Ashley Cole is brought down off the ball harshly by Batistuta, Pierluigi Collina, the bald-headed, so-called best referee in the world lives up to his reputation and stands for no nonsense. Batistuta gets a yellow card. England, well-warned beforehand by the more experienced team members, are not rising to any Argentine provocation. Danny Mills will later say that his face was spat at several times during the game.

The referee is having a good game, whereas Beckham's flicks and shimmies are not on song, both teams seem nervous and the opening exchanges are tentative.

On 19 minutes, Darren Hargreaves, having been injured in an earlier accidental collision goes off, descending the stairs and leaving the stage. In his place comes Trevor Sinclair, who, having shuttled back and forth between England and Japan whilst admitting he didn't have what it took to be an international player, completes the journey up the stairs in reverse. If ever there was a time to answer your calling, to take to the stage, this is it.

Sinclair goes out to the left wing and Paul Scholes slots into the middle, alongside Manchester United teammate Nicky Butt. With another colleague in Beckham out on the right and Sinclair in his favoured club position, everything clicks.

Butt harries at the back, in front of the defence, Scholes prods, Sinclair and Beckham come to life and Owen covers miles up front, dragging the Argentine defence this way and that, opening them up. Slowly, very slowly, there is a realisation that England can play football, that they can, and are, beginning to dominate possession, keeping the ball in a way that makes the eleven who finished the game in Saitama seem like forgotten strangers.

Butt puts Owen through and he puts the ball through a defender's legs, only to see it come back off the post to anguished cries from the crowd.

Batistuta heads into Seaman's hands, but England keep pressing forward, Beckham prodding, taking all the free-kicks and corners to the customary wall of flashes. Just before half-time, Owen makes a run into the box and is caught by Mauricio Pochettino, who sends a willing Owen tumbling to the ground. There is silence, an appeal, and Collina, the best referee in the world, steps forward, blows and points to the spot.

Penalty.

Owen approaches Beckham but the captain sends the striker away and tries to place the ball on the spot. Pablo Cavallero, the keeper, is already there and is talking to Beckham, trying to unsettle him. Beckham turns away and bounces the ball. Collina and Simeone, the enemy from four years ago in France, combine to send Cavallero to his goal-line. As he retreats, Beckham places the ball on the spot and walks backwards. Simeone tries to shake Beckham's hand. Beckham sensibly turns away and ignores him while Collina clears the box.

Breathing heavily, hands on hips and glancing toward the bench, Beckham waits, intently staring at the ball as whistles, boos and cheers ring around the ground.

Beckham exhales.

He takes four steps forward, the bandy legs moving, the left arm rising straight, high into the air. It comes down to the horizontal with the fifth stride, and as the right foot connects, his whole body is angled to the left. In the crowd, everything slows.

The ball moves toward the keeper, barely rising from the ground. Flashes buzz around the ground. The ball goes past the keeper to his left. He slumps and it looks momentarily as if he might get some contact on it, but it goes past him. The crowd is silent for a split second, as if waiting for confirmation.

The net bulges at the back.

The stadium erupts again.

Beckham runs to the corner flag, arms outstretched.

He kisses the number seven on his shirt and tugs at it, yanking it up and down, eyes fixed on the crowd, the veins in his neck bulging and his mouth agape in the midst of an extended, vocal chord-stretching cry.

'YE-E-E-E-E-E-E-E-E-E-E-E-E-E-E-SSSSSSSS!

As he is mobbed by his team-mates, his eyes are fixed on the crowd, as if he is making a point.

'Yes!' I did it for you. All of you who booed me, all of you who said cruel things about me, my wife and my child, all of you that called me stupid and mocked my clothes and my hair and my voice and pried into my private life. I did it for you.

And they love him for it.

All around the ground people hug each other, jumping up and down, sending paper cups flying, spilling their contents. As the jubilant of England dance, thousands of beer-bellies jiggle up and down.

England 1, Argentina 0.

I punch the air to the consternation of the photographers around me and I feel more English than I have for a long time.

Argentina press but are denied by Campbell and then Seaman.

Two minutes of time are added on and the theme from *The Great Escape* starts up.

Juan Sebastian Veron takes an Argentina corner that Rio Ferdinand heads away.

As the referee blows to end the half, huge cheers follow and, as every armchair fan knows after having heard TV commentators say it for years, England have scored at one of the two most crucial times, just before half-time.

Simeone gets the handshake he was after as he and Beckham clasp hands in some kind of acknowledgment of each other as they leave the field, down the steps, off the stage.

The crowd rush to the toilets and for refreshments. The atmosphere in the dome is buzzing; part disbelief, part nerves.

'YES!'

The atmosphere inside the respective England and Argentine dressing rooms can only be guessed, but for the second half, Veron, teammate of three of the England midfield four at Old Trafford, a player who kept Nicky Butt out for long stretches of the season, who must have felt like he was lining up against his colleagues on the training ground, does not appear. Outplayed, he is replaced by Pablo Aimar.

Looking for a goal at the second crucial moment, just after half-time, Owen and Beckham both go close for England.

Ten minutes into the second half and the team becomes even more like Manchester United, albeit the one of a few seasons earlier, when Teddy Sheringham replaces Emile Heskey.

Scholes goes close with a spectacular effort from outside the box.

England are playing like they tried to prove they couldn't at Saitama, and I almost have to rub my eyes to make sure it's England I am watching. Argentina cannot get a kick of the ball, which England are hanging onto easily. A move of 17 passes finally sees Scholes pick Sheringham out on the edge of the box. Sheringham swivels and connects with a superb volley that Cavallero palms away for a corner.

This is magic!

Sheringham goes close again before Argentina finally wake up.

Now their turn to pressure, they win corner after corner and pursue wave after wave of attack. The England defence is commanding and Seaman pulls off two wonderful saves when he has to.

England hold out.

The clock in Sapporo has slowed and time agonises toward the whistle.

Somewhere, in the ranks of the Argentine fans and the bars of Buenos Aires, time must be racing. Sensing the desperation of the situation, the Argentine players' frustration is obvious and a slew of rash challenges flies in.

'You dirty Argy bastards!' cry the aggrieved English.

Argentina seem to be getting closer and winning every dead ball, every throw-in, every corner.

Campbell and Butt make saving tackles in the box.

Pochettino heads high and wide.

The band plays the theme from *The Great Escape*.

Mills concedes a corner. England are under intense pressure.

Pochettino heads straight at Seaman. He should have scored.

Argentina keep possession.

Mills concedes another corner.

Three minutes to go.

The whistles rise from the crowd.

Two minutes of stoppage time are announced.

Pulses race.

The whistles intensify.

Collina puts his whistle in his mouth.

Collina inhales and blows his whistle.

One-nil, to the Engerland!

Beckham goes to the crowd and is ecstatically greeted.

I punch the air again and am feeling very English.

All around the stands people hug each other, sing and dance. Unlike after the game against Sweden, the team go to the crowd this time and are warmly received. The air is punched over and over.

People stay in the stands for a long, long time, as if somehow unable to believe that England have done it – at last. Revenge has been taken for 1986 and 1998.

Arms aloft, they chorus.

'One-nil, to the Engerland.'

Beckham will later say that it feels much better than four years ago. In the crowd in Sapporo, it feels better than that. The Chapman family, Emi, Neil and Tim, have come from Hong Kong and speak in the same superlatives heard all around the ground, outside and on the way back to the station.

'Great! Tremendous! Brilliant!'

Simon and Jacqueline Wescott have paid £5,000 in flights alone to come from Trinidad just for this game.

'It was worth every penny – fantastic!'

James, Andy, Paul and Peter, dressed in red and white tails, have come from Jakarta.

'This is the best day of my life.'

The Argentine fans outside the ground are dejected, but not bitter. A group from Buenos Aires have no comment except to say it *was* a penalty. They grimace for a photograph, then shake my hand and wish England good luck for the next game.

Down the steps out of the stadium, the volunteer staff give high-fives and hugs to the English. English fans have never been this popular before. Two David Seaman lookalikes say that they kept us in it. Two Argentinians in pointed hats say they are sad and they really hoped the team could win for the people back home who are having such a hard time.

At the bottom of the steps down from the stadium, an Argentinian stands, his shirt off and draped round his shoulders, the crest facing forward. He holds a handwritten sign above his head. The sign has two outstretched hands, one from Argentina, one from England, clasped together and shaking. On his forehead is a black love-heart inside, which are drawn the flags of both countries. The message is clear. I stop and shake his hand, we give each other the thumbs up, slap each other on the back. With no common language, not a word is spoken and I continue walking. It feels really good, a moment of spontaneous, hand-drawn, low-budget internationalisation.

The Japanese supporters all file out – dressed in England shirts, faces painted. One wears an Argentina away shirt, an England scarf and has an England flag draped around his neck. On his head is a rectangular LED scoreboard which displays messages, topped by half a football and four small flags sticking upwards; the flags of Japan, Korea, England and Argentina. Programmable, the four sides of the screen flash 1970s technology, rotating different messages around his head. Tonight it says only 'ENG-LAND'.

Four Japanese women pose for photos. Easily in their thirties, one wears fluffy, red rabbit ears, another a red curly wig, topped by a gold crown, the other two, more sober in red and white mad-hatter hats, hold a Manchester United teddy bear. All are wearing England shirts.

The ebullience and optimism all around is summed up by Ashley White and Mark Dalimore from Nottingham. Now a minor television celebrity after his appearance on a local TV documentary, White is carrying a giant-sized model of the World Cup and Dalimore two huge red roses. White looks at the monstrosity he will later struggle to get into a taxi.

'We're going to leave this one here and take the real one home. Magnificent!'

In the happy line marching down to the stadium, a cardboard cutout of David Beckham, frozen as he kicked England onto Japan against Greece, hovers above the crowd, watching over them as he sends them happily home for the evening.

Sapporo Dome has finished its stint as a World Cup venue and will now have to go back to hosting meagre crowds. On the wall at the station, next to an official sponsor's poster, written in Japanese and the five languages of teams competing at the Dome, is an attempt to ensure that the crowds and the atmosphere return. 'Please come back again'.

The subway trains are packed. The vast majority of the passengers are

Japanese and the vast majority of those are England supporters. Very few of the supporters from the two countries so passionate about England can communicate, though attempts are made in lots of ways. Smiles are exchanged, hands shaken and halting conversations in English started. It is largely the perfect image of what international exchange should be, everyone making allowances for the lack of understanding on either side.

Three Englishmen in their twenties get on the train behind me and sit down and, obviously exuberant, start talking about how they are going to celebrate.

'I'm going to go mental!'

'I'm going to be so bad, the girls had better watch out!'

One of them sees a young Japanese woman glancing at them and in his Cockney drawl, the lasciviousness starts.

'Oi! Darlin', c'mon over 'ere then!'

He waggles a finger in her direction. She seems surprised to be called, but obviously inquisitive, moves a few steps in their direction. One starts the singing and the others join in.

'Get yer kit off, get yer kit off, get yer kit off for the lads!

'GET YER KIT OFF FOR THE LADS!'

The woman has no idea what is being sung, but it is plain from the aggression in the voices and the slurring of the words that they contain real malice.

My heart sinks, after all the goodwill, surely it's not all going to go wrong? I'm about to move in between her and them when a wave of people get on the train, pushing her away from them and back to her friends.

'Thank God for that,' she tells them, 'they looked really awful.'

In Oyogi Park, the crowd has already gathered when I arrive. The railings next to the road are again swamped by flag-wearing English and Japanese fans. There are no Argentinians in sight. There is more singing and more dancing and there are more nervous police lines.

The singing and the dancing, though noticeably more slurred and unsure than in the afternoon, is all good-natured. The police don't seem to realise this, though, and keep shunting people from one place to another. Keen to keep the crowd off the flower beds, they move them away. Keen to keep them off the pavements and roads, they move them away. Keen to keep them out of the fountains, they move them away. People are beginning to get a little fed up and concerns are voiced that if there is one stupid incident, the whole thing could go horribly, horribly wrong.

Some England fans get up onto the podium where some dancing statues stand and unfurl a flag they must have made in their hotel room. A huge flag of St. George, each white square has a word printed on it made from iron-on letters brought for just such and occasion.

'JESUS TOOK THE PENALTY'.

If ever there was any doubt, Beckham's transformation is complete, though I can't help wondering how many spare Bs, As, Ss, Ts, Rs, and Ds they must have brought.

Hostesses from clubs all over Sapporo have the night off as most clubs are closed, either to avoid any trouble or because the 7,000 strong police force drafted in to cope with expected trouble has scared most of the regular customers away. Bar owners in the city complain that the police are costing them money and that the reaction is heavy-handed. The hostesses, happy to have a paid night off, are drinking and mixing with the England fans, some of whom misinterpret their professional flirtations.

Some flirtations are not professional, though are just as skillfully dished out. Mayuko, a 19-year-old student, sees my press badge and demands I take her photo. She is wearing a camisole top, encrusted with a sequin Union Jack. She looks at the photo I have taken and then demands I take another to show her in a better light. She then takes my pen and writes down her mobile telephone number.

'Foreigners are cool. Call me later – for private reasons, not for the magazine.'

The police are now surrounding the statue podium, their uniforms include leg protectors from knee to ankle, making them look a little like stormtroopers.

A bus comes around the corner, marked with large football drawings and emblazoned with the words, 'Fever Zone'. Someone in the crowd yells.

'Beckham!'

The bus is immediately swamped. It can't turn the corner for the crowd, and though by now it is obvious Beckham is not on the bus, nor is anyone else for that matter, a young Japanese fan has jumped up onto the bumper and is holding onto the windscreen wipers, banging on the windows. He is joined by more screaming fans, all male, all Japanese, and the bus is completely surrounded, thumped and kicked. The police move in and for a moment things look as if they might get out of hand. Non-uniformed police are taking photographs and videoing the scene and one fan from Bristol, who later says his job is shoplifting, jokes that the DSS will go to any lengths to take your photograph. Somehow the bus is free to move.

A snatch squad appears from behind the toilet building on the edge of the park and leads one man away. There is a commotion as he and his friends protest and all of a sudden four or five English fans are within a yard or two of the fracas, fists clenched, eyes and veins bulging, ready for action. They realise the lad that has been grabbed is Japanese.

'I would have got stuck in if it was one of our lads.'

The commotion dies down and the police move everyone away. A plain clothes officer tries to move me on as I take photos. I show him my pass and say I am working. He speaks fluent English with a heavy American accent.

'Yeah, me too, but I think our guys are over-reacting, they're too nervous.'

The nervousness continues on one side and the celebration on the other. Inevitably, someone jumps in the fountain and is followed by dozens of others. The police make efforts to get them out, but at dawn, there are still some people there.

Most have gone home to bed, or to find somewhere for a drink, one or two games of five-a-side are still going when light breaks. Here and there in the park, people are sleeping soundly and safely in ones, twos and threes. All have ignored the offer of a free bed from the local Christian Association that was handing out leaflets, preferring to rest their heads on their bags until they can summon the energy to go on to the next game.

I get talking to two young women sitting on a bench under a tree. It turns out they are hostesses and once they learn I'm English, they begin their routine, enquiring about the darker professions at home.

'Is there a sex industry in England?'

'I believe there is, yes.'

'Do the girls use their mouths or do they use what they have down there?'

'I've never been, so I wouldn't know, though I believe if you pay enough you get to choose.'

'You've never been? Mmmh. Don't Englishmen go, then?'

'I believe some do.'

'And the ones that don't, do they just masturbate?'

'I believe some of them do, yes, as I'm sure Japanese do.'

'Oh no, Japanese don't masturbate. Well, maybe the men do, but Japanese women could never touch themselves, not down there, not with our hands. I could do it with a vibrator maybe, but I could never go with a foreigner, you're all huge.'

'I don't think that's true.'

'It is, you know, I touched a foreign customer on the leg once, and there he was, down to here.'

She touches me on the leg, a couple of inches above the knee.

'I'm sure he wasn't. If he was, I don't think it's normal.'

Her friend joins in. 'I think it is, you couldn't get one of those inside you, it'd go into your stomach.'

'Japanese men are only to here.'

She touches me on the leg again, several inches higher.

'That's if they're big. If they're not, they're only to here.'

She touches me again, this time as far up my leg as it's possible to go.

'Well, my wife is Japanese…'

They seem a lot less interested in me after I mention my wife, so I make my excuses and leave. It is light and most of the people left in the park are unconscious or merely sleeping. I get back to the hotel at 7 a.m.

After only four hours sleep, I eat a breakfast of Hokkaido *ramen*, famed for its corn and butter. The television news says that people partied all night in

Susukino, the entertainment district in town, and noted that there were international games of five-a-side being played in the park. There is no mention of any trouble. All of the shops have sold out of English newspapers.

It's another beautiful day and I have one last look in the park, which is slowly filling up. The shirts are again off, the cans of beer out, the games of football being played and conversations are going on between Japanese, English and Argentinian in a mix of English and sign language. There is no obvious resentment for the defeat and no obvious gloating over victory. Some English say they hope Argentina give Sweden a good stuffing, and we'll see you again in the semi-final in Saitama.

A group of young Japanese girls asks a group of Argentinian men if they can take their photo with them. They do so, then the Argentinian cameras come out, kisses are planted on cheeks and everyone takes home a souvenir.

I talk to four young girls next to the fountain. They must be 17 or 18. One of them is wearing a yellow cotton T-shirt printed with a purple box bearing an English slogan written in white:

DELICIOUS
Leave nothing at all
Eat me whole

I tell her its meaning, as easily misconstrued in Japanese as it is in English. I tell her to be careful.

'Mmmh. That's a bit dodgy, isn't it?'

'Just a bit.'

As I leave to make my way to the station, the girls have approached the group of kissing Argentinians who are obliging.

Here is the proof. Internationalisation, if only for the day, is doing very well in Sapporo, cosmopolitan city with international events.

There are no newspapers at the kiosks in the station either, the international folk having snapped them all up.

On the train to the airport, filled mostly with tired English supporters, we pass through the city and into the rare, lush green of the outskirts of Sapporo. The Dome becomes visible as the train whisks us efficiently on.

I hear a whistle – a steam train whistle.

I look around to see if the oddness has registered with anyone else, or perhaps I have imagined it.

The whistle toots again. Peep, peep.

The noise is electronic and piped through the carriage speakers. An electric train with a steam train whistle.

Nobody flickers.

At the end of three days of delirious excitement, nobody seems to care.

we are nippon

9

Give Me Back My Islands – Japan vs. Russia

George Orwell's 1945 essay, 'The Sporting Spirit', called sport, 'war minus the shooting'. At the international level, he called it, 'mimic warfare'.

In football, of all international sports, nationalism plays a large part. There is no international baseball to speak of, tennis and golf are individual events and the Olympics are dominated by individual track and field competition. Rugby and cricket have world cups, but football is the only competition that, from the qualifying stages, involves significant numbers of teams from countries on each continent.

Players have the chance to prove themselves against the best in the world. They must use their own skills, intelligence and physical prowess in tandem with other players from their country to try and defeat the opposing national team. They wear their national colours, march onto the field behind their country's flag and then sing their national anthem. If this isn't war, it's as close as we can get without casualties.

I had visited Hitoshi in Mohehitei before the game.

'Of course it's war. Players get rich playing for their club for money, but when they're playing for their country, it's war. Countries that hate each other think, "at least we can beat them at football." The first international was between England and Scotland, wasn't it? It's war, of course it is, that's the only reason football is so popular. It gives poor countries the chance to beat rich countries. Countries that hate each other can fight without killing each other. It is war without weapons.'

Alfred agreed.

'It's absolutely true that football is war without the shooting. There was a football war in South America, El Salvador vs. Honduras, 5,000 people or so died.' [1]

At the semi-final stage of Italia 1990, a British tabloid newspaper ran an article on little-known facts concerning the semi-finalists. One of those was that England had defeated all the other semi-finalists in a war within living memory.

Nationalism is nothing new to Japan and was not brought here by the World Cup. Echoing those sentiments, however, in the build up to the second Group H game, both Russian and Japanese politicians made much of the fact that Japan and Russia had been at war between 1904–05.

In May 1905, Japan's navy, using British-built battleships, sank most of Russia's Baltic fleet. This cemented Japan's naval supremacy in northeast Asia and until 1945, May 27 was celebrated as Navy Day to commemorate the victory. Japan claimed the Kuril Islands and large tracts of Sakhalin – all islands between Hokkaido and Russia – as part of the 1905 Treaty of Portsmouth which ended the war. In the last days of WWII, Russia grabbed them back and this remains a territorial dispute equivalent to that which exists over Gibraltar or the Falklands.

Before Japan played Russia at the Yokohama International Stadium on June 9, Russian 'ultra-nationalist' and one-time potential presidential candidate, Vladimir Zhirinovsky, said that whoever won should retain possession of the islands. A 4-0 win to Japan would return the four islands to them. A 1-0 win to Russia would give them Hokkaido or Okinawa.

Japan's very own supreme nationalist, Tokyo governor Ishihara Shintaro, had earlier said much the same thing, claiming a Japanese win would help claims to regain the islands. He went on to say that this was an excellent chance for everyone to celebrate their country and 'ethnic race'. This was to be achieved by a Japanese team with a Brazilian striker and a French manager who doesn't speak a word of Japanese. Ishihara said Philippe Troussier represented the worst aspects of white people and called him a 'second-rate bully'.

According to Alfred, though, football is a stupid way to settle international disputes.

'It would depend too much on the referee. Referees give stupid mistakes and we couldn't have one appointed by the UN. Anyway, Germany would beat everyone.'

By the time I arrive in Yokohama Station, having again risen late and feeling a little hung over, I am short of sleep and temper.

The station is the usual cacophony. Although there are signs using the four colours clearly marking which way people should go to find their correct entrance, several volunteer staff stand in their nylon raincoats, yell into megaphones.

'Keep moving please!'
'Customers with red tickets this way!'
'It's dangerous to stop!'
'Customers with blue tickets that way!'
'Welcome to Yokohama!'
'Customers with green tickets this way!'
'Please buy tickets for your return train journey!'
'Customers with yellow tickets that way!'

Nobody mentions anything about the media shuttle bus and when I approach a volunteer, I cause consternation by asking a question that she doesn't have a prepared answer for.

'Excuse me, where do the media shuttle buses leave from?'

There is a pause while a quizzical look pours over the young woman's face. It disappears as she realises I am speaking her language.

'Please look at your ticket and follow the appropriate coloured sign. What colour is your ticket?'

'I don't have a ticket yet, I have to pick it up in the media centre.' I show her my pass. 'Where do the buses to the media centre leave from?'

'You don't have a ticket?'

'Not yet. Where is the bus to the media centre?'

'Mmmh. Just a moment.'

In a flash, an English-speaking volunteer is beside the young woman, who returns to shouting politely through her megaphone.

'Can I help you?'

'Where does the media shuttle bus leave from?'

'Shuttle bus?'

'Yes, the media shuttle bus, where does it leave from?'

'Shuttle bus, mmmh, I don't know. I haven't heard about that.'

'Never mind, I'll find it myself.'

Thirty yards away from the main station exit, the media shuttle bus pulls out of the station concourse, away from a giant football boot kicking a giant football. The streets are a sea of blue as the bus makes the short journey to the stadium. I wish I'd walked with the fans.

The bus pulls around a corner, goes down a hill, through a gate where we have to show our passes and then into the cavernous bowels of the stadium. It is surprisingly quiet. I half-expect to hear the dripping of water and see moss growing on the walls, though the scene is more reminiscent of a multi-storey car park.

I get my ticket, which is again for the field, and change it for the tribune. I instantly regret it. The tribune is boxed in behind the VIP section, under a roof. There are speakers playing music, drowning out the noise from the crowd. The seats are two rows of fold-away chairs, some of which have small pieces of paper attached to them, each with a newspaper or media organization's name printed on it.

There is an acre of space between the stands and the pitch. The stadium is huge, but being multi-purpose, complete with runnning track, means the view for watching football is terrible. The players on the pitch warming up appear tiny. I am miles from the action and wish I was down on the pitch.

Feelings of national pride have been evident since the draw with Belgium. This was the first time Japan had taken a point from a World Cup game, putting them, fleetingly at least, on a par with some of Europe's finest and tallest. To a country that sees itself and its people as being small, this was measured as a huge achievement.

After the Belgium game, there were national celebrations. TV personalities, prominent public figures and politicians all stepped up to latch onto the mood of the country and say their piece.

Prime Minister Koizumi Junichiro is at the game. After being elected just over a year earlier in a landslide victory, his popularity has dropped. Koizumi, along with millions of others, has cultivated a new interest in football. A cynical, populist politician, there is no way he would miss this chance to ride a wave of national sentiment.

A huge Hinomaru is hoisted above the heads of the crowd. Completely filling the bottom tier of the stand, the flag is moved hand over hand over the heads of the crowd until it completes the journey from one side of the stand to the other.

Vangelis' 'Theme' music starts and the players walk out of the tunnel. The cheering becomes spontaneous and the volume increases. After the Russian national anthem there is generous applause and then the flags drawn by the nation's schoolchildren are hoisted above the heads of the crowd. More so than in Saitama, there is hardly a space in between the flags as the sea of blue is replaced by one of red and white.

As the small, hand-drawn flags are waved above the heads of the crowd and they sing the national anthem, 'Kimigayo', Koizumi's face appears on the giant screen. He gets enormous cheers. He surveys the crowd and the legions of flags, big and small, lofted high over the heads of the nation he leads. This a man whose favourite book is a collection of letters by kamikaze pilots written before their fatal missions. A man who visits Yasukuni Shrine to pray for the souls of those that died fighting for the emperor. A man who loudly and proudly sings the national anthem.

Kimi ga yo wa,
Chiyo ni yachiyo ni
Sazare ishi no,
Iwao to nari te,
Koke no musu made.

Thousands of years of happy reign be thine;
Rule on, my lord, till what are pebbles now
By age united to mighty rocks shall grow
Whose venerable sides the moss doth line.

How much the flag and anthem mean to most people is hard to tell. To some it is a very sore point.

The flag and anthem were officially recognised by the Japanese parliament in August 1999. Japan's constitution states that the people, not the emperor, are the sovereign power and many pointed out that glorifying the emperor's reign was incompatible with this. The flag causes resentment as it was the symbol used by Japan during the war and is regarded as a symbol of aggression in Asia. Many left-wing politicians pointed out that both

Germany and Italy no longer use their wartime flags.

Many people claim not to know the words to 'Kimigayo'. Based on a Heian Period (AD 794-1185) poem, so antiquated are the lyrics that to grasp their meaning is tricky, a bit like trying to understand Chaucer.

After the law came into effect, the Education Ministry issued an edict calling for the hoisting of the Hinomaru and singing of 'Kimigayo' at graduation and admission ceremonies at all state schools. This was in response to the initial refusal of a high-school principal in Hiroshima to do so. In a dispute with teachers at the school and local education chiefs, he was ordered to comply. Rather than acquiesce, he committed suicide.

'Kimigayo' is often translated as 'His Majesty's Reign' and is the equivalent to 'God Save the King', since a female cannot ascend to the Japanese throne. The anthem was taken up after Englishman J. W. Fenton urged Japan to adopt a national anthem. Some claim Fenton wrote the original music in 1869, which was then adapted by imperial musicians. Others claim it was written by Hayashi Hiromori in 1880.

Whatever the truth, the cheers for Koizumi are resounding and in this national stadium, near the capital of the country, there is a whiff of nationalism in the air.

Whether this nationalism is of the kind to do Koizumi and Ishihara any good will only be seen between this and the next World Cup. The crowd, after singing 'Kimigayo', bursts into the anthem that is theirs, the one that extols the virtues of a newer Japan. A meritocratic Japan, overseen by the worst kind of white man, a second-rate bully.

'Troussier Nippon!'

'Troussier Nippon!'

'Troussier Nippon!'

The Ultras Nippon, the fanatic Japanese supporters with Italian names, the famously best-behaved fans in the world, the ones that tidy up after themselves, are a little more subdued than normal. Every Japan home game before the World Cup had been characterised by their particular brand of cheering. Behind the goal, Ueda Asahi, their leader, would occupy his usual position at the front of the stand, facing the crowd. Standing raised above them, his lieutenants to his left and right, he would conduct the singing and the playing. There were trumpeters and drummers. Directed by Ueda, the lieutenants would relay the chants he chose to the crowd through their megaphones.

Everyone would follow their cue.

'Ni–*pp*on, oh-oh-oh Ni–*pp*on, you can Nippon, you can Nippon!'

The last word followed by a drum rhythm counting 1-2,1-2-3-4-5!

On the last repetition of four, the drums and trumpets drop out, so that for a moment the stadium would seem eerily quiet, though filled with 70,000 voices, many of them female, many of them young, all of them in studied chorus.

'You can Nippon, you can Nippon! You can Nippon, you can Nippon!'
The drums come crashing back in: 1-2,1-2-3-4-5!

This time though, due to a FIFA edict, all flags on poles have been banned. The Ultras would normally hoist huge flags on poles up into the air and down again. Dozens of flags would line the perimeter of the stand and be hoisted in sequence, one up while the one next to it went down, creating a constant wave-like motion.

At Japan games there is constant motion and constant sound. At this level, the Japanese have not yet won, but they have always sung. Nobody could accuse the Japanese of only singing when they are winning.

The FIFA call to say 'yes' to children by the women with the Mickey Mouse voice is applauded. A voice screams through a megaphone, heard above everything else. The lieutenants follow, the crowd answers the call and takes up the chant.

'Oh, oh-oh-oh, oh-oh, oooh-oooh-Nippon!'

'Nippon, Nippon, we are Nippon!'

'Hey, hey, hey-hey-hey-hey!'

The referee puts the whistle in his mouth, looks several times around him and blows.

F-F-F-F-FLASH!

The stadium lights up as the moment is recorded for posterity and the game starts.

The crowd cheers everything. Every pass made, received or throw-in given. The merest hint of a chance is greeted by a noise that suggests it might win the game, no matter that it has just started.

Inamoto, hero of the opening draw against Belgium, gets the game's first chance. After four minutes, he tries his luck from about 30 yards, but his effort drifts well wide. What is really nothing more than a hopeful stab is greeted by a huge cheer.

Two minutes later Nakata Hidetoshi is fouled and Suzuki misses Inamoto's headed flick from the resultant free-kick. The crowd again goes mad. Expectations are high and the response is much louder than one would expect from a more football-educated audience. Perhaps Takeuchi is right, and most people here are not football fans, but Japan national team fans. Japan fans.

In between the photographers' tribune and the VIP section is a small corridor where people are milling around. VIPs are still taking their seats: Old men and women who look as if they don't have a clue what day it is, much less what is going on, where they should look or what strange game it is that is being played. They sit over-dressed and pompous, conspicuously at odds with the fans.

Escorted to their seats by pretty young women wearing blue uniforms with the appearance and demeanour of air-stewardesses, the VIPs lord it over them, holding up empty cups for refilling without once making eye-contact, letting it be known who is boss.

Most of them won't have paid for their tickets themselves and are being entertained at the expense of the sponsors and the people who buy their products. Some of the VIPs are asleep before the half ends. They snore in seats paid for by people in the stands and the thousands more who couldn't get tickets and are locked out.

Russia go very close with two efforts after 20 and 25 minutes. The crowd don't seem to realise it, but Japan are riding their luck. The referee, perhaps influenced by the fervour in the crowd, is giving every decision to the home side.

Nakata Hidetoshi blazes over an empty goal, Narazaki dives at Ruslan Pimenov's feet and Toda clears an Andrei Solomatin cross.

The game is being played end-to-end. The noise in the crowd doesn't abate, even when Russia go close. As half-time approaches, the Russians have more possession, but they can't convert it into solid chances. The Japanese hold on and there are no direct threats on goal as some VIPs make an early dash for the bar or the toilet.

When the second half kicks off, the VIP seats are still only two-thirds full and the pleasant young women lead a stream of old men to their seats, as the Russians again look to take control. In a repeat of the first half, they can't make their possession into clear chances.

Six minutes into the half, Inamoto strikes.

Released by Nakata Koji and Yanagisawa, Inamoto looks relaxed, not to say offside, as he receives the ball inside the Russian penalty area. He takes it down and calmly slots it away. He will later say on television that he thought he was offside, and was hence unhurried when he hit the ball.

Offside isn't given and Inamoto sets off on a celebratory run, pointing at Ono this time, before he is mobbed. Pandemonium breaks out as the stadium erupts into huge cheers. The replay on the screen and the subsequent announcements in Japanese and English get the same response.

Russia look for a quick reply. Egor Titov shoots wide from 30 yards. Vladimir Beschastnykh has an open goal after rounding the keeper, but hits the side netting from a tight angle.

Russia continue to go forward, but Japan don't give them any time on the ball. Nakata directs midfield traffic. He makes a run from midfield and his powerful shot hits the bar from 30 yards.

Nakayama 'Gon' Masashi comes on to a huge cheer. He wears his and the nation's heart on his sleeve and runs all over the pitch, hassling and harrying the Russians as they pour forward, looking for an equaliser.

With five minutes to go, Inamoto is substituted and receives a standing ovation.

The stadium is tense as the clock ticks down the last five minutes. Whistles echo around the stadium. People stand up, unable to sit. The cheers and drums are louder.

'Oh, oh-oh-oh, oh-oh, oooh-oooh-Ni–*pp*on!'

Boos for every Russian touch, cheers for Japan and chants of 'Ni–*pp*on!' cancel each other out, merging into a crescendo. Some look away, unable to watch. On the cusp of making history, the tension is palpable.

Nakata and Toda both fly into frantic challenges.

The final whistle is finally blown. Japan have made history, winning their first World Cup game. The team on the pitch and the crowd in the stands are ecstatic. The bench jumps up and then disappears in hugs.

The crowd unites in a loud cheer. Hands clap together, then shoot out in front of them as the cry is raised.

'Ni–*pp*on!'

'Ni–*pp*on!'

'Ni–*pp*on!'

Troussier slaps Nakata playfully on the cheek and the team take the applause from the crowd to a volley of flashlights.

The arms in the crowd shoot over their heads in a more traditional celebration.

'*BANZAI!*'

'*BANZAI!*'

'*BANZAI!*'

Sometimes misinterpreted as something more sinister, something that perhaps would be shouted during a battle for an island, the cheer is innocent.

'HOORAY!'

'HOORAY!'

'HOORAY!'

The hand-drawn flags are raised again.

On the way out of the stadium, the volunteer staff line the exits. They smile, wave and cheer.

'*Omedeto gozaimasu*! – Congratulations!'

'*Otsukare sama deshita*! – Thanks for your hard work!'

Further down the steps, down from the huge stadium that stands, almost sinister, elevated above them, they give high-fives and shout in English.

'YES!'

The reply comes back in Japanese.

'Ni–*pp*on!'

'Ni–*pp*on!'

'Ni–*pp*on!'

The crowd moves to the station. The stations are packed, but everyone waits patiently, some holding their hand-drawn Hinomaru. Another *banzai* is chorused. All over the country, people gather and chant for their team and country. In Osaka, people are jumping into the canal.

The battle is won.

The Road to Yokohama   Match 2   June 6 to June 11

Group A

June 6 France 0 0 Uruguay
Busan
June 6 Denmark 1 1 Senegal
Daegu

	P	W	D	L	F	A	GD	Pts
Denmark	2	1	1	0	3	2	1	4
Senegal	2	1	1	0	2	1	1	4
Uruguay	2	0	1	1	1	2	-1	1
France	2	0	1	1	0	1	-1	1

Group B

June 7 Spain 3 1 Paraguay
Jeonju
June 8 S.Africa 1 0 Slovenia
Daegu

	P	W	D	L	F	A	GD	Pts
Spain	2	2	0	0	6	2	4	6
S. Africa	2	1	1	0	3	2	1	4
Paraguay	2	0	1	1	3	5	-2	1
Slovenia	2	0	0	2	1	4	-3	0

Group C

June 8 Brazil 4 0 China
Seogwipo
June 9 Costa Rica 1 1 Turkey
Incheon

	P	W	D	L	F	A	GD	Pts
Brazil	2	2	0	0	6	1	5	6
Costa Rica	2	1	1	0	3	1	2	4
Turkey	2	0	1	1	2	3	-1	1
China	2	0	0	2	0	6	-6	0

Group D

June 10 South Korea 1 1 USA
Daegu
June 10 Portugal 4 0 Poland
Jeonju

	P	W	D	L	F	A	GD	Pts
South Korea	2	1	1	0	3	1	2	4
USA	2	1	1	0	4	3	1	4
Portugal	2	1	0	1	6	3	3	3
Poland	2	0	0	2	0	6	-6	0

Group E

June 5 Germany 1 1 Ireland
Ibaraki
June 6 Cameroon 1 0 Saudi Arabia
Saitama

	P	W	D	L	F	A	GD	Pts
Germany	2	1	1	0	9	1	8	4
Cameroon	2	1	1	0	2	1	1	4
Ireland	2	0	2	0	2	2	0	2
Saudi Arabia	2	0	0	2	0	9	-9	0

Group F

June 7 Sweden 2 1 Nigeria
Kobe
June 7 Argentina 0 1 England
Sapporo

	P	W	D	L	F	A	GD	Pts
Sweden	2	1	1	0	3	2	1	4
England	2	1	1	0	2	1	1	4
Argentina	2	1	0	1	1	1	0	3
Nigeria	2	0	0	2	1	3	-2	0

Group G

	P	W	D	L	F	A	GD	Pts
Mexico	2	2	0	0	3	1	2	6
Italy	2	1	0	1	3	2	1	3
Croatia	2	1	0	1	2	2	0	3
Ecuador	2	0	0	2	1	4	-3	0

June 8 Italy 1 2 Croatia
Ibaraki
June 9 Mexico 2 1 Ecuador
Miyagi

Group H

	P	W	D	L	F	A	GD	Pts
Japan	2	1	1	0	3	2	1	4
Russia	2	1	0	1	2	1	1	3
Belgium	2	0	2	0	3	3	0	2
Tunisia	2	0	1	1	1	3	-2	1

June 9 Japan 1 0 Russia
Yokohama
June 10 Tunisia 1 1 Belgium
Oita

10

I am Superstar – David Beckham

After Osaka Supporters Club made the origami crane flag for Beckham, the media swooped. The flag was unveiled at their Abeno ground and the next day, Takeuchi was all over the world's media, holding the flag. Calls came in from English radio, newspapers and television and Takeuchi jokingly described his elevated status to me in an email.

'I am superstar.'

The real article, though, was not in Osaka, but a short distance away in Tsuna-cho on Awaji Island.

Japan has not worshipped at the feet of an angelic English idol for years. Not since four mop-tops stepped off a plane and played at the Budokan in the same month England last won the World Cup, has the nation been quite so obsessed with an Englishman with a strange accent and unusual haircut.

At the 2002 World Cup, David Beckham's star was the one that outshone all others. From the moment he arrived, every move he made, every high-pitched squeak he let out, was scrutinised by the media and his hordes of adoring fans.

There were rumours that his stylist adjusted his hair at half-time. The stories about the writing on his boots – the name of his wife, child, tournament and his use of the Japanese exhortation *Gambatte!*, endeared him to fans as much as his tattoo and his easy, gentle way with people, particularly children. He is handsome, a great footballer, has a famous wife and a family he obviously dotes on. He is the perfect media star and in part, perhaps completely, the reason for the huge popularity of England in Japan.

On Awaji Island near Kobe, where England were based for the duration of the tournament, the locals took England to their hearts. They got their hair cut in the shape of the St. George Cross, opened an England football museum and put a handmade gold lion on the roadside. England thanked them by asking for a 14-feet high fence to be built around the training pitches so no one could see in.

Local restaurants served food in the colours of St. George and the team were followed by an enthusiastic crowd wherever they went. They were mobbed on a visit to a department store in nearby Kobe and had to be ushered into a side room where at least one squad member tried to take advantage of his popularity, fondling a female staff member and giving her his hotel room number.

After the Denmark game, Beckham called his popularity in Japan 'amazing' and put hope in millions of Japanese hearts when he hinted that he may like to finish his career here.

A conversation between two high school girls in Osaka Dome highlighted just how many of the England fans were Beckham fans. One girl told her friend that she would be really sad when the World Cup was over.

'Why?'

'Well, we won't be able to see Beckham any more.'

'What do you mean?'

'He won't be on television, unless you get satellite.'

'Why not?'

'Because you can only see the English Premier League on satellite.'

'Eh? You mean he doesn't play in the J.League? I can't believe it!'

Beckham would return to England, and when he did, the Awaji Westin Hotel, where the team were based, was flooded with calls from women wanting to sleep in his bed. The hotel put a ¥5,000 (£25) premium on rooms the England team had used and served a Beckham breakfast, the sushi he had requested every morning. Business at the hotel is booming and sales of Beckham shirts have not dropped since the tournament ended.

When the camp closed, a raffle was held to give away the things the team left behind. One excited woman held a T-shirt she had won and sniffed it.

'Ah, it smells of Beckham. What a nice smell.'

A man with her sniffed it.

'No, it smells like the manager to me.'

'Agh! No! It's Beckham! Beckham! Beckham!'

Perhaps because of his injury, Beckham didn't show his best in Japan, but this did not dent his popularity. The media and his fans credited him with creating Sol Campbell's and Rio Ferdinand's goals by virtue of taking the corners. Takeuchi, as ever, was not impressed.

'When Campbell scored it was a great goal; not because Beckham took the corner, but because it was a well-timed header. All the Japanese papers said it was Beckham. All the Japanese fans thought Beckham was great because of that, but it was just a normal corner.

'Against Argentina the Japanese fans were pleased because Beckham scored, not necessarily because England won. All the daft Japanese girls were shouting, "Beckham! Beckham! Beckham!" everywhere you went, there were loads of "Beckham 7" shirts, even at games when England weren't playing.'

Takeuchi also thought both England and Beckham were over-hyped.

'They were really lucky, the goals coming like they did. I was expecting more from them, but they aren't an interesting team. They are not spectacular or fantastic in any way, they have no entertainment value whatsoever.

'Beckham? What was Beckham doing against Brazil? He's not a player like Gascoigne who can turn a game. He can only cross.'

When England left Awaji, thousands turned up to see them off. The mayor announced that in commemoration of their stay, the town would erect statues of Sven-Goran Eriksson, Michael Owen, and, of course, Beckham.

Eriksson said he was proud of his team and thanked everyone. Beckham had a special word for his legion of Japanese fans.

'We thank Japan as a nation because the way they've supported us has been amazing.'

we are nippon

11

Welcome to Osaka –
England vs. Nigeria, Japan vs. Tunisia

Osaka is known nationwide for being different. People sound different, they eat different food and they think differently to the rest of Japan, as anyone will tell you. The Osaka dialect and accent are as instantly-recognisable as, say, Geordie or Scouse, and the effect they produce is at first one of fear, as it sounds terrifying, apparently, then humour. Osakans are regarded as natural wits and a high percentage of famous comedians originate here. The people are also regarded as being friendly and down-to-earth, unlike their near-neighbours from Kyoto, whom the Osakans regard much in the same way as the old clichés term the Japanese themselves: They are snooty, inscrutable snobs who spend all their money on clothes and finery.

Osakans, however, are violent thieves who spend all their money on food and alcohol, have the highest crime, unemployment and homelessness rates in the country and have a reputation for being ruthless in business. Posh Kyoto cake shops sell out by noon, thus ensuring their exclusivity. Osakans find this unbelievable. Traditionally, Osakans greet each other by saying, '*Mokarimakka?*' Which means, 'Are you making any money?' The pre-determined response is, '*Bochi-bochi denna* – Yes, I'm making a bit.'

Snow Brand, an Osaka dairy and meat company, recently had its unscrupulous production methods exposed. Milk cartons that were half-empty, unsold or past their sell-by date, were returned to the company and placed into vats to be recycled into new products. A second scandal occurred after it was announced that BSE had been found in Japanese beef. Home-grown beef is prized above all foreign meat and has a resulting high price. To protect the industry, the government announced it would compensate companies against the losses that resulted from the ensuing destruction of all meat. Snow Brand, ever keen to reply favourably to the local greeting, relabelled and repackaged beef imported from Australia as Japanese, then threw it away and made a claim for compensation. Just after the World Cup, Universal Studios Japan, a theme park in which the local Osaka municipal government is the major shareholder, was exposed for selling food past its sell-by-date at its restaurants and pumping untreated industrial water to its drinking fountains.

Osaka is home to a fine castle and two football teams, Cerezo and Gamba. Most people follow the Hanshin Tigers baseball team more fervently, and this is in part where the city gets its rowdy reputation. In 1985, when the Hanshin Tigers last won the Japan League, fans gathered in the city centre and jumped off bridges into the filthy Dotomburi, the canal which flows through the south of the city. They removed the figure of Colonel Sanders from a nearby Kentucky Fried Chicken outlet and threw him in, too. The Colonel is now chained to his post.

Osaka's Nagai Stadium, specially renovated for the World Cup, is home to J.League Division Two team Cerezo Osaka. Three games are to be played here; Nigeria vs. England, Japan vs. Tunisia and a quarter-final, which, all things being highly unequal, could be England vs. Japan.

Both Takeuchi and I express similar sentiments about going to see England play at Nagai. It's almost unbelievable. I have been here for seven years, Takeuchi for sixteen. Non-J.League football of any quality is very hard to come-by in these parts. In 1996, I saw Newcastle humbled 3-1 by Osaka Gamba on a day when it was too hot to sit down, never mind run around. Other than a couple of Japan friendlies, the thirst for top-level football is slaked by the English, Spanish, Italian and German leagues in the early hours of the morning via satellite television. One of the more comforting thoughts that occurred to me when preparing for the afternoon kick-off in Nagai was that all over Europe, people would be forced from their beds at an ungodly hour, as I am often for mid-week Premier League games.

This time Takeuchi has a ticket, though not from the British Embassy.

'I heard that the Nigerian FA were selling tickets, so I called the number of a Nigerian support group in Tokyo. They confirmed they were selling them. All the Nigerians were going home and they wanted to make some money, that's what they're like. Look at the shoplifting Senegal player – no matter how you look at it, he's a thief. A thief plays a match, scores a goal and he's in the papers. The shop that he stole from gives him a present for spreading the shop's name all over the world. It's bizarre, but that's Africa. They wanted some pocket money, I guess.

'They were openly selling tickets for ¥30,000, they weren't hiding it at all. "¥30,000, please. OK, here's your ticket." It was good for me, though, if I'd bought one somewhere else it would have cost more. My friend picked the tickets up from the hotel where the team were staying.'

The rainy season has started, it's official. The newspaper says the Meterological Agency announced that, after starting in Kyushu on Monday, the rainy season arrived in Honshu on Tuesday. Looking out of my window on the Wednesday, across the roofs of the houses below my apartment, past the Christmas-tree-shaped cone of flashing lights on top of the local *pachinko* parlour over to the low range of Ikoma mountains that mark the border of Osaka and Nara, there is nary a cloud in the sky. It is 29°C (84°F).

Any Japanese will tell you the country has four distinct seasons. The

World Cup supporters,
mind your manners!

世紀の祭典
WORLDCUP
サポーターはマナー
を守ろう！

UNITED NATI

Simon

Takeuchi not

Pak

Shintani

Hitoshi

Alfred

Top: Saitama cheers Nakata Hidetoshi. **Above:** Rainy season damp squib at Miyagi.

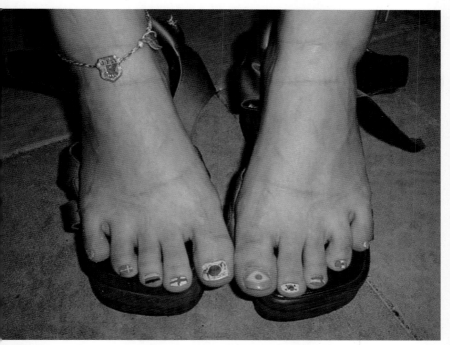

Top: The World Cup on your feet at Brazil vs. Belgium, Kobe. **Above left:** Mr. Scoreboard Head flashes, 'Morishi!' **Above right:** Samurai celebrate a point in Saitama. **Centrespread:** Faces of the 2002 World Cup in Japan.

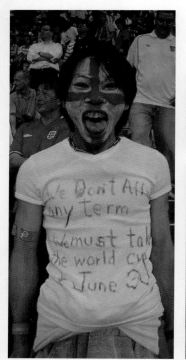

Top left: C'mon England! **Top right upper:** Saitama Stadium sits in the fields.
Top right lower: Victory to Japan! **Above:** Troussier Nippon! Losing celebrations in Shibuya, Tokyo.

Above: Made in Japan – Japanese England fans in Shizuoka. **Below left:** Nakata Hidetoshi directs traffic before taking a corner.
Below right: 'Taxi for Beckham! Taxi for Beckham!'

The blue tide flows home.   ALL PHOTOGRAPHS © SIMON MORA

television and newspapers delight in reporting when the seasons start and end and how many days late or early they are. In spring, the news programmes feature the progress of the 'Cherry Blossom Front', which they map as it brings the warmer weather and blossoming trees up from the south. On a given day, the staff uniforms of Japan Railways (JR) change from winter to summer weight and the drink machines that stand on almost every corner change from selling hot drinks to cold. Given the reluctance of the weather to adhere to the official timetable, this can leave short-sleeved JR guards shivering on chilly spring evenings, unable to find a drink to warm them up.

I walk out of my house, leaving my umbrella behind. Not only is it unlikely that it will be needed, but FIFA, in its wisdom, while holding the tournament in the middle of the rainy season, has banned all but collapsible umbrellas. At the discretion of security staff, umbrellas may be confiscated at the stadium gates. Official World Cup™ rainwear will, naturally, be on sale.

I get on the subway, just like I do when I go to work, except today I'm going to see England play Nigeria. Changing at Shinsaibashi to the Midosuji Line, there are lots of English fans, adding to the abnormality of it all. It is as if a London Underground train has taken a wrong turn and arrived in Osaka, forcing me to deal with the pasty and lumpy of Ealing as well as the noisy of Osaka.

The subway, which normally has announcements in Japanese and English, has added French for the duration of the qualifying tournament, it may yet have to add Chinese, Portuguese, Spanish, Swedish, Turkish, Danish, Russian or Arabic. It's a safe bet that most have been prepared. The special announcement tells people which station to get off and guides them, via the colour on their ticket, to the appropriate exit.

A Japanese couple from Tokyo sitting next to me don't hear the announcement, so I tell them which station it is that they want. They are surprised to hear me speak Japanese, particularly with an Osaka accent. As usual, this attracts staring Japanese eyes. Today, the English stare at me, too. An oddity every day because I am an Englishman on a Japanese train who speaks Japanese, I now appear equally odd to the Englishmen who I ran away from and who have followed me here.

Getting off at Nagai Park and walking round to the media centre, I am sweating. After picking up my ticket, I sit and fan myself for a while and start up a conversation with a visiting American journalist. Most Osakans, I tell him, don't get too far from the air-conditioning on days like this.

In the park beside the stadium, the now familiar ritual of international exchange is taking place. I linger longer than I should, taking photographs and swapping stories with Nigerians, Japanese and white, black, Asian and expatriated English people. Most of them seem to work in marketing.

Although surrounded by a running track, Nagai is a good footballing venue, where there is a knowledgeable football crowd. The stadium is packed and England are again the home team.

After the success against Argentina, England expects again and the atmosphere inside the ground is good. Away to the far left of me a Nigerian band are playing Fela Kuti-style rhythms, which they will keep going for the whole match. England lose out in the style and swagger stakes again.

This doesn't detract from the support though, and even the announcer who goes through the team sheets can't disguise his excitement. After finishing the Nigeria list rather flatly, he raises his voice to twice the volume.

'And now – *England*!'

Cheers erupt all around Nagai Stadium and thousand of cameras capture Beckham's face up on the screen.

The teams come out to a great reception, the national anthems are respectfully observed, only slightly marred by the English again missing their cue. The cheers and shouts build to a crescendo. The referee checks his watch and with the linesmen and then blows his whistle. For the next 45 minutes, nothing happens.

England are absolutely awful. They play like there is nothing at stake, like it is a midweek, meaningless friendly. The only real action is the battle of the bands in the stands, a contest the Nigerians win hands down.

The band play well, but not enough to keep Takeuchi amused. He is sitting in front of the band amongst the Nigerians that have stayed in Japan and a host of people who have also visited the Nigerian FA.

'I want my money back. This is rubbish. It's Nigeria's last game, they are on the way home, so it doesn't matter to them. That's fair enough, but England have to avoid losing. The support for them is the same, but they don't look like they want to win. They look like they can't be bothered.'

England wake up just before sending Takeuchi to sleep. Owen shoots wide and Scholes has a shot parried onto the post, but England are wholly unconvincing.

Nobody can see how close Owen and Scholes went because FIFA has decided that replays can't be shown on the big screens, fearing they may incite the crowd. They might also give a closer glimpse as to how bad some of the refereeing decisions are.

Half-time comes none too soon and the crowd rushes to buy beer. In front of the camera positions, three Geordies are throwing beer and water around and have obviously been drinking since breakfast. The cameraman next to me, aiming past them at the crowd on the opposite side of the stadium, receives a mouthful from one. He looks ridiculous, his Newcastle shirt tucked into his very short, white nylon shorts as he acts hard.

'The dentists in Japan are very good.'

There has been no trouble so far, but the aggression is still there, as it was in the bars of Osaka the previous night. One English fan looked Alfred's girlfriend square in the face and told her in no uncertain terms what he'd like to do to her, making the point that it was to, not with her. There were various inquiries of, 'What're you looking at?' and an air of suppressed aggression not normally seen in Osaka has come to visit. I rather hope it goes away again soon.

The second half brings much of the same. The speedy Julius Aghahowa breaks for Nigeria and the skillful Jay Jay Okocha threaten, but both times Ferdinand is masterful at the back. Owen fails to get a touch on a Heskey cross and then Sheringham shoots well over on 75 minutes.

The game peters out. Both sides seem happy to play for a draw. The England Supporters Band doesn't seem to care and they play Ant and Dec's awful 'On the Ball', drowning out the Nigerians. It ends 0-0, which means England are through in second place. If they progress, they are now likely to meet Brazil at the quarter- not semi-final stage.

Outside the ground, I meet Takeuchi. He says he's having the time of his life, the World Cup having come to him, but it hardly shows.

'I know it's hot and that's hard, but they are professionals and we've paid a load of money to watch them. We made that flag for Beckham and gave England, the team and the consulate loads of support. We wanted to see a great game in Osaka. That game was Beckham's reply? He didn't try at all. They would have lost without Seaman and Ferdinand and they could have been out.

'There was no variation in their play, it was boring. If they really were playing for a draw, they should have used Sheringham and Vassell from the start and rested the others, but they used the normal starting line up. Do they really think they'll progress like that?'

Takeuchi can't join me, as he has to go off somewhere else, but I meet up with the British Embassy football team and several journalists down from Tokyo.

We trawl through Osaka's many nightspots and keep running into the same groups of TV crews, journalists and photographers looking for a story, looking for the English hooligans. Thankfully there are none and though rowdy, the night in town passes off with no more incident, possibly even less, than on a normal Friday or Saturday night.

In one bar, a Scotsman tells me he was supporting Nigeria, and that he is sick of the English. Far better, he says, to be Scottish.

'The best thing about being Scottish is not being English.'

I tell him I think this sounds sad. If there is not enough about being Scottish to make him proud, that if the thing he can celebrate most in his nationality is that it means he is not the thing he despises most, it's a damning indictment of Scotland. Besides, their football team are useless.

'Listen to you. Did the English win the World Cup in 1966? We've never stopped hearing about it. You just can't forget about it.'

I ask him about the Scotland fans that chant songs about Bannockburn when Scotland play England.

'That's different, though, that was a battle.'

Two days later, Takeuchi again has a ticket. He has had anonymous phone calls for days offering him the chance to buy. The most expensive price was ¥120,000, about £650. In the end he paid ¥50,000, around £270, more than eight times face value. His expectations are as high as the price he paid.

This is his day, his stadium, where Cerezo, his team, play week in, week out. Something of a minor media celebrity since OSC made the England flag for Beckham, Takeuchi is on local television in the morning with Yusef, a Tunisian who lives in Osaka. Yusef says that if Tunisia don't score twice, they won't go through. Yusef predicts 2-0 to Tunisia and Takeuchi 1-0 to Japan.

The prime minister, is also on the news, saying he will stop work at 3.30 p.m. and support the Japanese team. A man on the streets of Osaka, asked what he thinks of this, says it's fine.

'It's not as if he does anything anyway.'

Businesses are allowing their employees to take the day off to watch the game, or have put TVs in the office. At the Tokyo Stock Exchange, the dealers are wearing the blue of the Japanese team.

On the trains to Nagai Park, outside and inside the stadium, after the victory over Russia, most people are a little more confident than Takeuchi was.

'2-0, easy. We'll get to the semis!'

'3-0, we can win the whole thing!'

Perhaps it's just the park, or that the sun is shining, or that the location is familiar, but the atmosphere at Osaka seems somehow different. Less serious and yet more sincere. The Osakan sense of humour is even shown by the people holding up signs for tickets. Not the cardboard of Saitama and Yokohama, the Osakans hold up their 'tickets wanted' requests written in white tape on blue, transparent, inflatable Lilos. A higher percentage of the costumes and accessories on show are handmade.

Inside the ground there are empty seats again. JAWOC is blaming FIFA and FIFA is blaming JAWOC. The atmosphere is great, though, and the stadium is much better than Yokohama.

When Troussier's name is announced, he gets a huge cheer. The man's popularity has shot up and the crowd put his name before their own when they chant.

'Troussier Nippon!'

All the world loves a winner.

During the national anthem, far fewer people in the crowd hold the small Hinomaru flags above their heads. Though 'Kimigayo' is well sung, it is clear that this is more than a patriotic event – people are here to cheer on the football team. Takeuchi is equally clear on the matter.

'Flags? We don't need those flags. Adidas are giving away the Miyamoto mask, though. What the hell are those flags drawn by little kids, anyway?

What do they do with them afterwards, throw them away?

'It's good to see the big flags when Japan play here, but I wouldn't want them at a Cerezo game. If I see the flag when Japan aren't playing, I just wonder if it's a national holiday.'

Just before kick-off, the noise in the stadium, though the capacity is only two-thirds of Yokohama, is by far the loudest, most frenzied yet. Later on television, the players will say that at half-time they could not believe the noise.

Every section of the crowd sings and if the noise drops, allowing the voices of the few Tunisian supporters here to be heard, a voice screams through a megaphone to get the chant going again.

'Troussier Nippon! Troussier Nippon!'

Everyone joins in.

In the heat of the afternoon, neither side really gets going. Japan make their neat triangles work in the middle of the field, though not with any penetration and Tunisia, though needing to score two to qualify, seem happy to simply contain.

The crowd, meanwhile, are annoyed with the Tunsian goalkeeper. One of his defenders is taking his goal-kicks, for which he gets a thorough booing.

The voice strains through the megaphone again.

'Yanagisawa!'

The whole stadium joins in.

Over 30 minutes have been played before the first goal attempt. Yanagisawa shoots from 20 yards, but Ali Boumnijel in the Tunisia goal gets down well to save. Japan are doing a passable impression of England. Again, the support is second to none, but perhaps the stadium is jinxed.

At half-time, the score remains nil-nil and Takeuchi has a confession to make.

'I can't believe it – I fell asleep! It was hot, boring and I fell asleep in my seat behind the goal. I was knackered. It was looking like it was going to end 0-0. I came to support Morishima, but he didn't play the first half. I slept for about 15 minutes. At half-time, my mate, another Cerezo fan, woke me up.'

As the crowd realise Morishima Hiroaki will be playing for the second half, the noise level goes up. This is Morishima's home stadium and many of his home fans are here to cheer him. A megaphone isn't necessary.

'Morishi, Morishi, Morishima!'

'Morishi, Morishi, Morishima!'

'Morishi, Morishi, Morishima!'

Japan attack straight from the kick-off, getting into the Tunisia penalty-box. Suzuki tears down the right, is tackled by Raouf Bouzaene, but the ball breaks loose to Morishima – he drills it in from 12 yards. Nagai Stadium explodes.

'Ni–*pp*on! Morishi!'
'Ni–*pp*on! Morishi!'
'Ni–*pp*on! Morishi!'

Japan get stuck in. They play with a passion that England lost a long time ago. I wonder how the match would have gone if England and Japan had met here in the quarter-final, which is now impossible. I wonder how it would have gone and who I would have supported. It would have been a close-run thing. If I had to judge on the passion in the football, the good nature in the crowd and which fans I'd be happier for, I don't think I'd be singing about being English till I die.

Nakata Hidetoshi mimics Beckham and spoons another free-kick over the bar.

Japan buzz around Tunisia, Nakata, Morishima and Ono all causing problems. Ichikawa, the other half-time substitute, gets free down the right and sends in a hanging cross which Nakata heads down and through the keeper's legs to put Japan two up.

Tunisia hit the bar, trying to spoil the party.

The game is over as a contest, but with seven minutes to go, Morishima runs 40 yards to keep a ball in play ten yards outside the Tunisian box. He exemplifies the pride all the players seem to show when playing in their national colours. Like England, Japan is a country where you are instantly recognised by your accent and people take huge pride in their region, though they seem to fall far more easily under the banner of nationhood than do the English.

The Osaka crowd boos the Tunisian substitutions.

Two minutes later, Nakata goes off and all bridges seem to be mended as he hugs Troussier, the man he famously fell out with last year, the man who said he was too big for his boots.

At the full-time whistle, the noise is louder than bombs and the bank of flashlights blinding. Nakata gets an enormous cheer when he is announced man of the match and the whole crowd lift their arms above their heads.

'*Banzai! Banzai! Banzai!*'

Outside the stadium, the police form lines across the street and shepherd people across the road. A crowd gathers at the end of the road that leads from the stadium, as people begin the long wait for the team bus to come out.

Back in the park, there are no Tunisians around, and Japan enjoys its moment in the sun.

The subway trains are suspended because of a fault on the line and the station staff have to fend off angry complaints.

'Has someone died? Hurry up and get the bloody thing fixed, I've got to get home.'

'I've bought a ticket, are you going to give me my money back or what? Get it sorted out, this is Osaka's busiest line!'

While I'm taking photos outside the station, I bump into Takeuchi. He is so hoarse he can hardly speak, although he manages to bark at a security guard who tries to move us along.

'I could cry! When I knew Morishima was coming on for the second half, the atmosphere was great. It was all Cerezo around me – normal supporters. When we were shouting for him, he scored. It was like it was the Japan fans were at the end opposite us and we were the Osaka fans, the Cerezo fans. We were louder.

'When Morishima scored, I cried. Our Morishi, the guy we always support, playing at our stadium, scoring the kind of goal he never gets – and because of that goal Japan qualified. I jumped a mile out of my seat and burst into tears. I was over the moon. I feel like crying now when I remember it. I've already forgotten Nakata's goal, but I'll never forget Morishima's.'

Another man who cried was the prime minister, Koizumi. Trying to again milk the moment, he said tears welled up in his eyes when Japan won. Koizumi had earlier in the year sacked Foreign Minister Tanaka Makiko from his government. Tanaka was very popular, and Koizumi had used her popularity to get himself elected. When he fired her, she cried. This prompted him to say that tears were a woman's greatest weapon.

The trains are soon running again and I go to Ebisu Bridge, the favoured spot for leaping into the canal. The police have already cordoned the bridge off, but the sound of repeated splashes can be heard. This side of the lines, complaints are being made and any excuse tried.

'Come on, let me through, let me through, I left my mobile phone over there.'

'My friend has my money and he's waiting for me on the bridge.'

The police let them through. It looks easy, so I show my press badge.

'It's work, I have to get through and take some photos or my boss will fire me.'

'Sorry, we can't let anyone through.'

'But you just let those two lads through.'

'I'm sorry, but you can't go through.'

'Come on, I'm not going to jump off and get my camera wet, am I?'

'Sorry, no.'

'But...'

'No!'

The crowd is packed tight against the police lines. A young man on his friends' shoulders leads the crowd in song.

'Troussier Nippon! Troussier Nippon!'

The mood is undoubtedly celebratory, but this is perhaps not the sort of patriotism Koizumi would prefer to see. In magazines and newspapers, young people say it is the first time in their lives that they feel proud, really proud, to be Japanese. They have worn and hoisted the flag for the first time with meaning, rather than it being forced upon them at school ceremonies. It means something to them now, because it is theirs, this is a new kind of patriotism that they have created. A new Japan where, as in the football team, old notions of seniority count for nothing. If you're good enough, you're in. You can even get in if you're foreign, like Alex, the Brazilian, or the Frenchman whose name, in this new form of nationalism, comes before the name of the country.

'Troussier Nippon!'
'Troussier Nippon!'
'Troussier Nippon!'
'Troussier Nippon!'

I have to leave to go and meet Pak in Korea Town, where we will watch Korea play Portugal on a big screen in the park. The crowd stays, though. Stays and keeps jumping off the bridge, some people in swimwear, some in their underwear and some wearing nothing at all.

Later on television, Inamoto, an Osaka native, is asked to comment on the fans' unruly behaviour. Japan's new hero captures the mood perfectly when he says that if he were there, he'd jump in, too. Takeuchi says Inamoto is stupid for saying it and that the fans who jump into the river are not real football fans, that they are immature. Takeuchi may be right when he says they aren't football fans, he calls them 'just Japan fans'. He may be right about that, too. There is a definite feeling that the young have put a new slant on being Japanese. They are expressing it through their support for the only team they have that can compete on the international field with any competency.

There are arrests. One man for driving his scooter into the police lines and one young fan for indecent exposure. His friends later turn on the police and hurl fireworks at the nearby police box.

'Troussier Nippon!'
'Troussier Nippon!'
'Troussier Nippon!'
'Troussier Nippon!'

12

Korea Town – Korea vs. Portugal

Osaka is home to the largest population of Koreans in Japan, with around 180,000 residents, 90% of whom have South Korean nationality. When Japan annexed Korea in 1910, thousands of Koreans were brought to Osaka to work in heavy industry, doing the so-called 3-K jobs – *kitsui*, *kiken* and *kitanai* – difficult, dangerous and dirty – that the locals didn't want to do. As subjects of the Japanese empire, these people were regarded as Japanese, though without the basic legal and political rights of true Japanese. That all changed with Japan's defeat at the end of WWII, and while around one-third of the Korean population returned to Korea, the rest stayed and found themselves no longer Japanese, but Korean residents of Japan.

All Koreans born in Japan are entitled to permanent residence and are, naturally, obliged to pay tax. They cannot, vote, however, and are unable to claim some benefits because they are technically foreigners.

To naturalise and become Japanese, a Japanese name must be taken, though a small minority have won the right to keep their Korean names through the courts. The Koreans that stayed in Osaka congregated in a district called Tsuruhashi in the city centre and this is now a thriving Korean market and restaurant area.

Pak was born in Sakai, Osaka, to ethnic Korean parents, his grandparents having come from Korea to Japan during the Korean War. Brought up in Japan, although educated at a school for Koreans and fluent in Korean, Pak claims he doesn't know what his nationality is.

'I don't really know whether I'm Japanese or Korean. I was brought up in Japan, this is home and I was brought up as a Japanese-Korean. I feel Japanese, but if I'm asked my nationality, I say Korean. If someone else said I was Korean, I wouldn't really feel I was. I wouldn't want to live in that horrible place – it wouldn't suit me.'

Many Koreans are teased and bullied as children because of their names. Though Pak has never taken a Japanese name, he was only ever teased as a kid for being crap at football.

Arriving from Ebisu Bridge, I meet Pak, my wife Kumai and Seinoski, another OSC member, at Tsuruhashi Station and we take a taxi down to a park in Momodani.

I remind Pak that when I asked him before the World Cup started who he would support, Japan or Korea, he said he couldn't decide. Now he supports Korea first and Japan second.

'But that's just because I'm contrary, if everyone around me says they support Japan, I don't want to be the same. By supporting Korea, perhaps I'm confirming that I'm Korean, though I don't really know. When I've been watching Korean games I find myself jumping in the air when they score, but when I support Japan, I don't.'

The reaction to the success of the Japanese team has been fantastic, but in Korea, looking from Japan, it is as if a new religious cult, all dressed in red, has taken over the country.

The sight of millions of Koreans on the streets has amazed the Japanese, who, though by and large patriotic and proud, don't consider themselves to be anywhere near as parochial as the Koreans, who they see as aggressive nationalists. Pak, too, is astounded.

'When I first saw the reaction in Korea I thought it was amazing. The Koreans' football was typical of them, though, really direct. The players have really gone for it this time. Hiddink has had a huge influence, he's given them self-confidence. I don't know as far as skill goes, but they have confidence and I think that makes a difference.'

It has to be said, too, that the Koreans have been in four World Cups and lost every game, so there was no way in their opening match against Poland that they would want to be outdone by the Japanese, who had got their first World Cup point in only their second tournament half-an-hour earlier. Korea duly beat Poland and 1.5 million people celebrated on the streets of Seoul.

Ahn Jung Hwan is Korea's answer to David Beckham or Nakata Hidetoshi. He plays in Serie A, has permed hair and a model wife. When he scores he kisses his wedding ring. Against the USA, he reveled in taking revenge for an incident in the winter Olympics in Salt Lake City in February 2002.

An American speed-skater, Apollo Ohno was awarded the gold medal in the 1,500 metres after Kim Dong-Sung of Korea, who had finished ahead of him, was disqualified for blocking Ohno on the final lap. There were furious protests from the Koreans and Ohno received death threats by email from Korea in such volumes that they caused the official games website to crash. When Ahn equalised for Korea against the USA, he mimicked a speedskater when celebrating his goal and later confirmed he had dedicated the goal to Kim.

'We knew that our people still have a grudge against the United States for the skating, so we wanted to allay that with the goal ceremony.'

This displayed a strong sense of nationalism, keenly felt and evident not just on the football field or streets before and after matches, but in the furious responses to websites or newspapers that denigrate Korea in any way. Soccerphile.com, a 2002 World Cup website, received thousands of emails, including death threats, after running a piece seen as disparaging Korea. On the first day of the tournament, *The Japan Times* sacked its senior sports editor in response to furious protests from the Korean Embassy after he wrote a piece painting Seoul in a less-than-favourable light and mentioned Korean prostitution. Koreans are often portrayed on television in Japan as protesting on the streets, burning flags and slitting open fish that represent Japan in a comment on a long-running fishing dispute.

The USA team, though, was apparently amused by the skating routine, one player even saying it was a nice gesture. Pak doesn't think so.

'That was stupid, it had nothing to do with football. The Americans had maybe forgotten about it, but the Koreans hadn't.'

In the park, the rain isn't dampening the small crowd's spirits. Very much a local event, like a summer festival, there are food stalls set up around the small park, selling the Korean favourites *kimchi* – spicy pickled vegetables – pickled squid and *chijimi*, a kind of savoury pancake. Children and dogs run to and fro and a very drunk elderly Korean man, Korea flags poking from the bandana he has wrapped around his head, is leading the children sitting on plastic sheets in front of the screen in Korean song and dance.

'*Oh, pil sung Corea* – Korea must win!'

'*Oh, pil sung Corea* – victory to Korea!'

This song too, has Pak irked.

'When people say '*Dae Han Min Guk*', in English, it would be Korea. They sing '*Oh pil sung Corea*', which they then spell with a C if they write it down. It's really stupid, it should be a K, but they spell it with a C so that it comes before the J of Japan. It's ridiculous, they should spell it with a K.'

I get the feeling Pak would be lynched if he went to Seoul.

There are several camera crews from the local television stations in the park. They stand on either side of the screen, the lighting technicians higher up on small steps. Every time there is some kind of reaction in the crowd, the lights go on, so the cameras can record it for their Japanese audience. The camera lights are so bright that nothing can be made out on the screen. This, the rain and the attraction of *kimchi*, *chijimi* and beer distracts me from paying too much attention to the game.

My own brand of nationalism means that I have one eye on the other game being played that evening. If results go the right way and Poland beat the USA and Korea and Portugal draw, the USA will be out.

After only 25 minutes, João Pinto is sent off for a reckless lunge at Pak Ji-Sung. Though Korea pour forward, the news that the USA are two down dampens the urgency in the crowd.

Robert Luis Beto is sent off for his second bookable offence on 66 minutes and then, two minutes later, Park, a player with J.League team Kyoto Purple Sanga, scores a cracking goal. Taking the ball on his chest, he flicks it past a defender with his right foot and in one sweet move, volleys an unstoppable shot with his left. The home crowd in Incheon, where the game is being played, goes crazy, as does the small crowd in Tsuruhashi, which is then blinded by the television lights.

Portugal suddenly remember how to attack and push forward with their remaining nine players, Figo goes close with a free-kick and Nuno Gomes misses when it seems easier to score. Korea hold out to win and both crowds again go mad.

I buy celebratory beers and we all learn some more Korean from Pak.

'*Mansei! Mansei!*'

'*Banzai! Banzai!*'

'Hooray! Hooray!'

The match leaves a bad taste in the mouth when the Portuguese claim the referee was influenced by the crowd. Ahn counter-claims that Portugal had tried to fix the game, telling Korea they should play for a draw so both teams could go through together. This led to bad feeling on the pitch, he says, which culminated in Pinto's early dismissal for his tackle on Park. Pinto was later banned by FIFA for punching the Argentinian referee Angel Sanchez in the stomach.

As Portugal fail to equalise, despite losing 3-1 to Poland, the USA go through to the second round, to Seinoski's obvious delight and the disappointment of just about everyone else. Even when the people of different countries argue, they can usually agree on at least one thing. Everyone wants the USA to lose.

We leave and stop in at Mohejitei on the way home. Hitoshi says Figo was unlucky with his free-kick and then he claims to have forgotten that we had a bet.

'It was only ¥1,000, come on, pay up.'

'Alright, I'll take it off your bill.'

The television news says that more than 500 people have jumped off the bridge in Osaka. They are waving their flags and shouting, 'Nippon! Nippon!' The country is caught up in a celebration of patriotism.

The Oi! singer I'd met before, Mikku, is in Mohejitei, though he isn't too happy.

'I don't think that the manager should be a foreigner,' he says of Troussier.

Hitoshi points out that the crowd don't seem to agree, given that they are shouting, 'Troussier Nippon!'

'Those young kids at the games with the Hinomaru round their necks are really ambivalent about their country,' he adds, 'they're told not to sing the national anthem at school. The best football teams in Japan are near Tokyo and in Yokohama. Maybe the people in Yokohama like the flag, maybe that's what's important to them, but not in Osaka.' Hitoshi points at the television. 'They are just copying what everyone else does.'

I ask Hitoshi what he thinks of the Koreans.

'The people at the Korean games don't care about football. They just go there to enjoy the World Cup, they just want their country to win, they hate other countries.

'They're like murderers. If there was a war, the Japanese would run away because they don't have confidence in anything. The Koreans would fight.

'Because of the situation with North Korea, they are educated to be prepared for war. We are educated for peace. They are educated, brainwashed if you like, into thinking that we are their biggest enemy.'

Hitoshi then runs through a story that is often heard in Japan about why they are different to most of the rest of the world.

'In Japan, we are from an agricultural background, the Koreans are hunters, that's why they are bigger, stronger and can act individually. We farmers are smaller and have to act collectively.'

Mikku bristles and he and Hitoshi get into an ethnological debate.

I have to plan my trip to Niigata, so I leave them to it and go home to bed.

The Road to Yokohama   Match 3   June 11 to June 14

Group A

June 11 Denmark 2 0 France
Incheon
June 11 Senegal 3 3 Uruguay
Suwon

	P	W	D	L	F	A	GD	Pts
Denmark	3	2	1	0	5	2	3	7
Senegal	3	1	2	0	5	4	1	5
Uruguay	3	0	2	1	4	5	-1	2
France	3	0	1	2	0	3	-3	1

Group B

June 12 S.Africa 2 3 Spain
Daejeon
June 12 Slovenia 1 3 Paraguay
Seogwipo

	P	W	D	L	F	A	GD	Pts
Spain	3	3	0	0	9	4	5	9
Paraguay	3	1	1	1	6	6	0	4
S. Africa	3	1	1	1	5	5	0	4
Slovenia	3	0	0	3	2	7	-5	0

Group C

June 13 Costa Rica 2 5 Brazil
Suwon
June 13 Turkey 3 0 China
Seoul

	P	W	D	L	F	A	GD	Pts
Brazil	3	3	0	0	11	3	8	9
Turkey	3	1	1	1	5	3	2	4
Costa Rica	3	1	1	1	5	6	-1	4
China	3	0	0	3	0	9	-9	0

Group D

June 14 Portugal 0 1 South Korea
Incheon
June 14 Poland 3 1 USA
Daejeon

	P	W	D	L	F	A	GD	Pts
South Korea	3	2	1	0	4	1	3	7
USA	3	1	1	1	5	6	-1	4
Portugal	3	1	0	2	6	4	2	3
Poland	3	1	0	2	3	7	-4	3

Group E

June 11 Cameroon 0 2 Germany
Shizuoka
June 11 Saudi Arabia 0 3 Ireland
Yokohama

	P	W	D	L	F	A	GD	Pts
Germany	3	2	1	0	11	1	10	7
Ireland	3	1	2	0	5	2	3	5
Cameroon	3	1	1	1	2	3	-1	4
Saudi Arabia	3	0	0	3	0	12	-12	0

Group F

June 12 Sweden 1 1 Argentina
Miyagi
June 12 Nigeria 0 0 England
Osaka

	P	W	D	L	F	A	GD	Pts
Sweden	3	1	2	0	4	3	1	5
England	3	1	2	0	2	1	1	5
Argentina	3	1	1	1	2	2	0	4
Nigeria	3	0	1	2	1	3	-2	1

Group G

June 13 Mexico 1 1 Italy
Oita
June 13 Ecuador 1 0 Croatia
Yokohama

	P	W	D	L	F	A	GD	Pts
Mexico	3	2	1	0	4	2	2	7
Italy	3	1	1	1	4	3	1	4
Croatia	3	1	0	2	2	3	-1	3
Ecuador	3	1	0	2	2	4	-2	3

Group H

June 14 Tunisia 0 2 Japan
Osaka
June 14 Belgium 3 2 Russia
Shizuoka

	P	W	D	L	F	A	GD	Pts
Japan	3	2	1	0	5	2	3	7
Belgium	3	1	2	0	6	5	1	5
Russia	3	1	0	2	4	4	0	3
Tunisia	3	0	1	2	1	5	-4	1

we are nippon

14

A Train Through the Hinterland – England vs. Denmark

Takeuchi had bought a ticket for the round-of-16 game at Niigata that turned out to be England vs. Denmark. As his domestic strife increased with his continued absence from home during the World Cup coupled with not having enough money, he passed the ticket to ladies' man Shintani.

The previous night, after I got back late from my encounter with Hitoshi, Shintani and I had an exchange of emails where we discussed the best way to get to Niigata.

Niigata lies on the Japan Sea Coast, 364 miles and seven hours by normal train from Osaka. We agree that the Shinkansen is too expensive and decide to take the Thunderbird instead. The Thunderbird is an express train that used to be called the *Raicho*, which was written in kanji characters. Raicho actually means Thunderbird, but the English name, everyone agreed, sounded much better.

I had eventually got to bed at 4 a.m. and when I rise four hours later, I again make a note that this has to stop. I get to Osaka Station to meet Shintani a little after nine.

We buy tickets, consulting the JR timetable, a directory that is bigger, weightier and has smaller print then the average British phone book. Shintani, not surprisingly, makes a mistake and we only just make the 9.42 Thunderbird bound for Toyama.

Shintani is more talkative than I've ever known him and we discuss politics, the British Empire, Thatcher and Blair before moving on to the essential differences between Asia and Europe. Shintani, an engineer, tells of his wonder at seeing the stone buildings of Rome when in Italy to watch Nakata play in Serie A.

'When we visited the old buildings we were amazed. "Look at that, the walls are stone! Oh, the floor's stone too! Look, the roof's stone and the walls are at 90° to the floor!"'

I say I had similar thoughts on seeing my first Buddhist temple in Thailand, with a 90-metre reclining Buddha and that to most Europeans, the huge, wooden temples of Nara and Kyoto are equally impressive.

'I mean, they're all wood.'

'True, but Japan only uses concrete now. When there were no roads and Japan was re-building, the old prime minister, Tanaka Kakuei, came to an agreement with the building companies. They wanted jobs, so they agreed to build the roads, railways and dams. Part of the agreement was that for every cubic metre of concrete poured in Japan, half a yen would go to the Liberal Democratic Party (LDP), which they still get now. It's called a political contribution.'

This must explain, I say, why Japan seems able to put up concrete white elephants in the most remote backwater, almost overnight.

'It's not law, just an agreement between the party and the building companies who are all run by the yakuza. The yakuza are all builders. They get jobs from the government and give them votes in return.'

On our way over miles and miles of concrete worth millions and millions of yen to the LDP, Shintani and I are internationalising well.

We stop at Toyama for lunch and when we ask directions to the bank at the station information centre, the woman directs us and then asks if we are going to the match. We reply that we are and I ask her who she is supporting.

'England, of course!'

That a middle-aged Japanese woman in a small town in the countryside would declare her support for England seems at once strange yet a given. Such is the support for England, the whole country, I get the impression, feels the same.

We are almost a week into the rainy season, which is characterised by high humidity and intermittent, often very heavy showers, but can also be quite cold, particularly in the mountainous regions which are often shrouded in mist. The rainy season is also the time when the rice fields are planted.

Today it is cold and grey and though the humidity is high, Shintani and I are shivering in our shorts and T-shirts. After a brief lunch we set off down what seems to be Toyama's main street, to buy some raingear or trousers. We find a cheap place but neither of us, no matter how cold it was, would stoop to buying anything there.

The walk out in town does illuminate one thing though: Shintani does seem to have an eye for the ladies, or at least the young, uniformed schoolgirls that seem to be everywhere this Saturday afternoon.

Shintani's eyes dart this way and that at schoolgirls in groups of two and three, some with plain, navy skirts below their white blouses, others with maroon check skirts, all improbably shortened. Loose socks, socks up to the knee, held there with 'sock glue' and yet loose around the ankle, are still popular, several years after their first appearance. Wide-eyed and jacketless, we leg it back to the train.

From Toyama, we soon leave the built-up outskirts of the town and are surrounded by newly planted rice-fields. Shintani soon does what most Japanese seem to do a few moments into a long journey and promptly falls asleep, his head forward slightly, bobbing around. Any jerk or twist of the train, rather than waking him or nudging his head onto my shoulder, sees him automatically adjust his position so that he remains seated, facing forward, almost as if saying grace with his clasped hands in prayer over his groin.

The rice fields stretch on and on and then the landscape becomes increasingly mountainous and the open spaces narrow. Because it is officially summer – the calendar tells us – the air-conditioning is on and I am shivering in solitude. The train completes a huge loop to the right and the Japan Sea is visible out of the left-hand window. Away to the right are the rice fields. The rice is planted in rows about six inches apart and is still short enough for the water it lies in to be seen between the green shoots. Turning my head to the right and looking out of the train window perpendicular to the tracks, the rows of rice run away to the foot of the mountains. Looking straight over at the mountain, the light that permeates the cloud dances in a grey, muddy beam through the fields, following the motion of the train.

The train twists again and runs parallel to the coast. The fields still run away to the right, chased by the sunlight that the heavy clouds allow, catching up with the mountains, the tops of which are lopped off by the mist. The sea, rice fields and mist on the mountains. The perfect, woodblock print picture of Japan, and all this on the way to an England game.

Further on, the fields begin to give way to factories, building yards and *pachinko* parlours. Shintani, displaying another skill the Japanese seem to learn at birth, wakes just in time for us to get off and change trains. We get onto a two-carriage train, again seemingly in the middle of nowhere. The train is full of high-school boys on the way home from a school sports club. Shintani doesn't seem concerned as we pass through a station in the middle of yet another set of rice fields. At this station, a gaggle of high school girls waits on the opposite platform. Shintani remarks that the length of skirts in the countryside is significantly shorter than that in the city. I say that I can't believe that there is a football stadium anywhere near where we are. According to Shintani's earlier calculations, at 5.50 p.m., we should only be ten minutes away from Niigata Station.

Shintani asks a young woman sitting opposite us in a business suit, who seems as out of place on this rural train as we do, if we are on the right train for Niigata. She confirms that we are and Shintani gives me a knowing look.

'And will we be there in ten minutes?'

'Ten minutes? Oh no, it'll take at least an hour from here.'

'An hour?'

Shintani and I chorus, he in surprise, me in desperation. The media shuttle bus from Niigata Station will be leaving without me. I will be late again for the photographers' briefing, late even, for ticket collection. My phone, which has constantly been playing up, can get a signal, but the speaker keeps cutting out, meaning I have to wobble it around, opening and closing it, until the connection is made. It's rather a hit-and-miss operation, so I grab Shintani's phone and call the hotline that FIFA provide for no-shows or those arriving late, telling them in somewhat dramatic style that I have been otherwise unavoidably detained and will be late, but no matter what, hold on to my ticket. I don't tell them that I am shivering as I trundle through the countryside, underdressed, and accompanied by a famous ladies' man, who is ogling out the window at another gaggle of schoolgirls.

It is 7 p.m. when we get to Niigata Station, an hour later than planned. An hour and a half before kick-off, but 30 minutes before the waiting list starts to take tickets from the no-shows. I realise I forgot to get the name of the person I spoke to at the media centre, and start to panic, imagining the most horribly keen, yet inefficient do-good, busy-body imaginable, writing my name down incorrectly and then losing the piece of paper she wrote it on, giving my ticket to one of the thugs from the *Sun*, *Star* or *Mirror*. We get off the train and run up the stairs, Shintani runs off in one direction and I in the other, having arranged to meet on the platform for the 1 a.m. overnight train back to Osaka.

By the time I find someone who is not only prepared to speak to me in Japanese, but realises I am not a member of the public with an appropriately colour-coded ticket and can direct me to the bus stand where the media shuttle bus leaves from, it has, of course, already done so. Another member of the press is also there, easily identified by his surly manner, incessant pacing up and down and the ID card he is wearing around his neck. As it is 35 minutes until the next bus, I suggest we get a taxi together.

It turns out he is from Macedonia. We swap stories for a few moments before we are snarled in traffic. He tells me that the Germans beat Paraguay one-nil.

'But they do not enjoy their football. They play like a boring machine.'

The buses to the stadium, ferrying the members of the public with their appropriately colour-coded tickets to specifically colour-coded destinations down specially-laid-on bus lanes are speeding past us. I ask the driver if there is a quicker way to the stadium and he suggests walking, unless, perhaps the traffic is getting through on the by-pass, round the other side of the stadium, though that is difficult to say.

A voice comes over the two-way-radio, directing another taxi in another part of the city and I wonder, I say, if the office might know if the traffic is getting through on the by-pass. Our driver asks for any information and we get a reply – the bypass is clear.

'This is the sort of job I like,' the taxi driver says, 'Is it OK if I take the by-pass, it'll cost a few extra-hundred yen.'

'Go!' I shout, stirring the Macedonian.

'Go!' he joins in.

The taxi driver turns a sharp left and we take the by-pass, through empty lanes and soon we can see the Big Swan, though it still seems miles away. I suggest to my new friend that he call ahead to make sure his ticket does not go over the border.

We get to the stadium gate, only for the driver to take a wrong turn, necessitating a U-turn and adding another couple of minutes onto the journey time. The taxi driver is forced to stop by the gate security. As he doesn't have a stadium pass, he is told he shouldn't be on this road. I think for a moment that we are going to have to sprint but the guard hands the taxi driver a pass without so much as asking his name. He then checks our passes and we arrive at the media centre gate, pass through and get our tickets, 23 minutes before kick-off.

Inside, the stadium this time is completely red and white, though there are more red crosses on a white background than vice versa, indicating that England, and not Denmark, are again the home team.

Ten minutes before kick-off, a Mexican wave travels around the stadium, as the spectators play their part in the script. The chant of 'En-ger-land!' is as loud as the chants of 'De-en-mark!' are inaudible.

As the teams line up for the national anthems, the excitement builds and the stadium fills with noise. The camera scans the players' faces during another poor rendition of 'God Save the Queen'. When Beckham's face appears on the screen behind the goal to my right, high-pitched voices again scream out and camera flashes light up the stadium as fans take photos of Beckham's huge face as he sings.

Little attention is paid to the Danish anthem and the strains of 'I'm English Till I Die!' ring out, accompanied by the least rhythmic band I've heard yet, The England Supporters Band. Like the team they support – and the fans who support both them and it – the band make up for what they lack in natural talent, sparkling rhythm and dash and daring, by going at it all-out, lung-busting, hell for leather. It's not very pretty nor easy on eye or ear, but it's bloody effective. The whole stadium is alive in a celebration of red, white, Beckham and England. The sense of expectation is palpable.

As the whistle goes, the stadium erupts further, the organised cheering and repetition of simple lines changes to a more visceral, primal cry; the flashes again sparkle on all sides of the ground as Denmark kick-off, pass the ball backwards, as Heskey, Owen and Scholes close in, their determination obvious from the very start.

On four minutes, England win a corner to the left, diagonally opposite me. Beckham strides over to take it and a few flashes ping. As Beckham places the ball, steps backwards and swings the world's most famous bandy legs into action, the bank of flashlights is simply stunning; the brightest, lightest, biggest shock yet. I move back in my seat in surprise, startled at the wall of light that momentarily replaces the spots of red and white in the stands. I move my hand to make a note as Ferdinand rises and Thomas Sorenson, perhaps dwelling on the moment himself, or temporarily blinded by the flashes, scoops the ball up and puts it over the line.

One-nil to the Engerland!

This time I do manage to make a note: England have not yet scored a goal from open play.

England give the ball away with alarming ease, and by the end of the game, Denmark have enjoyed 63% of the possession and had ten shots to England's eight. This seems to matter not to the English fans who see Butt skillfully flick on for Owen to put England two up on 22 minutes.

Two-nil to the Engerland!

The replay reveals that the man Pele would later surprisingly label as the best player of the tournament, didn't play Owen in with the deft flick that was widely reported, rather the ball clattered him somewhat awkwardly, and bobbled into Owen's path. Regardless, Owen puts the chance away well, which encourages the England supporters and their band into a chorus, to the tune of 'Knees Up Mother Brown', of, 'We're not going home, we're not going home, we're not, we're not, we're not, we're not, we're not going home! Boom!'

A few minutes after Owen's goal, the rainy season offers up its best. The rain teems down in sheets and it's chilly, with the rain drumming on the Perspex roof of the Big Swan Stadium like a thousand miniature drummers disturbing the sleep of those inside a caravan or tent holidaying in the Lake District in July. As Shintani had pointed out earlier, the ball boys and girls stand at their posts, drenched, with no one saying 'Yes' for them. The English fans, under the expensive comfort of the Big Swan's roof, continue to the refrain of 'Knees Up Mother Brown'.

'We're not getting wet, we're not getting wet, we're not, we're not, we're not, we're not, we're not getting wet! Boom!'

Denmark, still being given possession far too easily by their opponents, squander a chance away to my right, with Thomas Sand shooting wide of goal after a good ball in from Thomas Gravesen, the game taking on the appearance of a combination of Manchester United, Liverpool, Leeds and Arsenal playing a combination of Everton, Bolton, Charlton and Sunderland.

Just before half-time, Denmark surrender possession from a Mills throw and Beckham pounces, feeding Heskey to his left, who, with customary power and lack of placement, blasts the ball so hard that, even though Sorenson gets some contact on it as it goes under his body, England go three up.

Three-nil to the Engerland!

An impromptu rendition of 'God Save the Queen' begins as fans return to their seats as the second half kicks off. With Fowler on for Owen, then a few minutes later Dyer on for Scholes, England are coasting, they and the fans thinking that the game is already won.

England keep possession, with only a yellow card for an over-reaction by Danny Mills, coming much later than anyone had expected in England's fourth game, and a fumbled shot and then clearance to worry them.

In the stands, the England supporters, the feared hooligans from before the tournament, have broken with stadium protocol and, whilst singing, 'Let's all have a disco, let's all have a disco, la, la, la, hey, la, la, la!' are doing the conga. Soon enough, all the sections and all the tiers of all the stands have joined in, the Japanese joining in with their new friends, these white, beer-bellied, shaven-headed strangers, the black Londoners, the Asian Yorkshiremen, the Singaporean Chinese, ex-pats from Trinidad, Hong Kong and Indonesia, hoist the local children onto their shoulders as Japan and England are joined together in a Cuban dance. If this isn't a summer festival, if this isn't fun, never mind the rain; if this isn't a half-drunken, badly-timed dance step on the dance floor of internationalisation, it will never happen.

The conga wears itself out and the chants turn to 'We shall not be moved.' At the final whistle, the celebrations on the pitch are matched by those in the stands. Friends and strangers hug and as the crowd trickles out, having seen their heroes off the pitch, the staff are there again, all smiles, congratulations and high-fives.

'Thanks for coming!'
'Thanks for your hard work!'
'See you again!'
'Bye! Bye!'
'*Ingurando*!'

Outside the stadium the singing and dancing continue as everyone moves slowly and happily to the buses to take them back into town.

Crowds line the route and cheer and take photographs when they see something or someone they think worthy of a souvenir, something to show their friends, something to record the night and prove that they were there.

At the station, the mingling, singing and celebration carry on, people wandering this way and that, between the bus terminal and the station, the hotel opposite, the bars and restaurants in the streets flanking the station, cramming into the nearby convenience stores to buy cans of beer.

On the zebra crossing, two thin, young Japanese women, one wearing a red, sleeveless cotton T-shirt with 'England' printed across the chest pose for a photograph and say they are going for a drink.

'We are going to celebrate,' says one, standing slightly back on her left heel, pushing her backside slightly out and her small chest slightly up, her cropped top lifting to reveal her navel.

They tell me the name of the °bar they are going to and suggest I join them, just as the sound of England comes crashing round the corner. The England Supporters Band having just got off a bus and breaking into a rhythm of sorts, play loudly as everyone follows, singing.

'We're not going home, we're not going home, we're not, we're not, we're not, we're not, we're not going home! Boom!'

Like rats following the Pied Piper, the fans fall into line behind the band, a few photographers running ahead, stopping and taking a few hurried shots before running ahead again to find another position.

The band march over the road, turn right and park themselves on the steps of the Tokyu Inn hotel and give an impromptu concert, running through their catalogue of celebratory numbers: 'We're Not Going Home', 'We're on the Ball' and the theme from *The Great Escape*.

The crowd gather below them and join in, singing and clapping. Everyone sings from the heart and with the best intentions, but the overall impression is one of a drunken crowd joining in at a sing-song in the local social club, as everyone does their turn. An excited, young Japanese boy, wanting to be as close to the action as possible, keeps mounting the steps, getting too close to the drummer for his liking. With his hand free in a semi-quaver between beats, he pushes the Japanese lad off the step below him. The Japanese lad stumbles down a step and turns to see who has pushed him, only to see a drummer intently drumming. He again goes up one step and the process repeats itself over and over.

A section of the crowd gather behind the band and raise flags across the door, giving them a background of St. George. A white, nylon wig, replete with red cross has been taken off and is waved in the air like a cheerleader's pom-pom. There are headbands, football-hats, wigs and costumes. Television crews relay the pictures back to the world's, or at least Japan's, TV sets, photographers snap away for tomorrow's headlines and calls are made on mobile phones, relaying the atmosphere to different parts of the country, perhaps even the world. The young Japanese men, who make up the majority of the crowd facing the band, wear England shirts or have the flag of St. George draped around them, cape-like. They wave their hands above their heads, keeping time; palms toward the band, their little fingers held beneath their thumbs, the usual two-digit 'peace' sign normally seen in photographs replaced by a new, three-digit one.

'Three-nil to the Engerland!'

An elderly couple stand on the edge of the melee.

'What's going on? What are they singing?'

Two Danish supporters are commiserated by England fans, both native and Japanese.

'We are very sad, is it OK if we cry? We were beaten by the better team, we'll support England now.'

A middle-aged Japanese man wears an England shirt, an England flag painted on his face, on his head a conical, straw hat of the type worn when working in the fields, this one customized with the England colours. Next to him a trio from London, wondering how long their money will last, stand in wigs and England shirts, one with a flag painted on his right cheek, a red line below his left eye and 'God' inexplicably written in red on his forehead. They will stay until the Friday at least, they say, but could stretch their money and budget if they have to.

'How much would you pay for a ticket if we get to the final?'

'I'd go to a grand, I reckon.'

'Me too, easy, I reckon we can do it, an' all.'

'We're on the ball, we're on the ball, we're on the ball, we're on the ball!'

The band finishes the gig and leave the steps of the hotel to thunderous applause and cheering, only to re-appear a few moments later on the terrace above, milking it for one last encore.

'We're not going home, we're not going home, we're not, we're not, we're not, we're not, we're not going home! Boom!'

I am, though.

I make my way back across to the station, having bought some beer and crisps – all that was left in the convenience store worth eating – and shuffle off a little reluctantly to meet Shintani. I wonder for a few seconds if I should try and find the girls in T-shirts who'd told me where they would be drinking, then I hurry away. I pass some English men chatting to some Japanese girls. Everyone's mind has turned to internationalisation, of one kind or another.

'How long in Japan?'

'Until Friday.'

'Mmmh. How about Japan?'

'Very nice.'

'Oh? How about Japanese?'

'Very nice, especially Japanese girls – beautiful!'

'He-he-he. Oh really?'

'Yes. Do you know a good place to go for a drink?'

'A drink? OK! Let's go for a drink together with us!'

When I get to the platform just after half-past midnight, it is already crowded. There are marks for each carriage door, where the train will stop precisely, and a queue emanates from each one, along the platform to the mark for the next carriage door, where it snakes back on itself in a big loop and carries on in the opposite direction on the other side of the platform. It is here I find Shintani, sitting down in the queue reading his World Cup guide and train timetable. His 'Owen 10' shirt, rarely off his back, is wet.

'That was a great game. It was easy for England, but Denmark were good after England relaxed. The supporters were a good laugh, doing the conga. I thought the fans would be more serious, that there would be a lot more serious chants and stuff. I hadn't expected to see them doing the conga and singing "We're not going home" in the rain. It was great, they looked as though they were really enjoying themselves when the Japanese fans joined in and copied them.'

Shintani and I share a celebratory beer, sitting on the platform waiting for the train back to Osaka. Shintani, like most football fans in Japan, was not taken in by all the hooligan hype.

'I didn't think any hooligans would be coming, none at all; that's old news. There were lots of people against England coming to Japan. They are the real hooligans, I think. The mass media here are weird, they brainwash the population, they think hooligans are going to riot and take over. It's nonsense.'

Shintani notes that I have emptied my first can before he has barely touched his.

'The bars could have made a fortune the way the English drink. They should have put flags in the windows, but the police told them to close down while England were in town. They just don't want the responsibility. The people who make these decisions are stupid.'

The train pulls into the station and all the unreserved seats disappear before we can get on. We settle for sitting on the floor between the first and second carriages, waiting to see if anyone gets off.

We meet a writer I know from Soccerphile.com, who sums up the feelings around Niigata as it sings and dances in the rain.

'It's a festival of fun.'

We all get seats and I sleep fitfully until the train pulls into Osaka at 9.30 a.m. I have spent 17-and-a-half hours of the last 24 on trains.

I go home and sleep for a few hours before watching Sweden vs. Senegal on television in the comfort of my own home. I've now been to eight games and have watched the rest in pubs or on television in the media centres. Kumai and I settle down on the sofa for a lazy Sunday afternoon as the teams come out at the Big Eye Stadium in Oita.

Kumai is sick of all the European teams winning and is supporting Senegal.

'It would be good if an African team got through. Besides, Sweden's yellow shirts get on my nerves and all their players are ugly.'

Larsson puts the Swedes in front and Kumai is not happy.

'Why do all their noses stick up in the air?'

Senegal have a penalty appeal turned down and a goal disallowed before Henri Camara equalises stylishly.

The game goes into extra-time and after chances at either end, Camara scores again and Senegal go through, celebrating with a dance.

'*Yokatta*! – That's good!'

After a couple of hours, Ireland in white play Spain in dark red.

'The teams in dark shirts look stronger. It's the same with Othello, black is always better.'

Spain take the lead.

'See?'

A sliding tackle flies in.

'The grass looks lovely, doesn't it? I'd like to have a picnic on it, it looks really comfortable.'

Ireland have more of the ball, but Spain are in control and have two goals disallowed for offside.

In the second half, Niall Quinn comes on and heads over on the hour. Annoyed with himself, he spits.

'Don't they get spit on themselves when they do sliding tackles? Don't they get spit on their strips, then notice when they're running down the wing and think, "Ugh, I've got spit on my sleeve!"?'

Ian Harte misses a penalty, but Ireland push forward and again Robbie Keane scores at the death through their second penalty. Ireland dominate the first period of extra time, though not so the second and it goes to more penalties.

Matt Holland, David Connolly and Kevin Kilbane all miss for Ireland, as do Garcia Juanfran and Juan Carlos Valeron for Spain. Steve Finnan scores with Ireland's last kick, but so does Gaizka Mendieta, taking Spain into the quarter-finals. The commentator says that Ireland were unlucky, apparently forgetting that the replays showed that at least one of Spain's disallowed was onside.

We both crash out on the sofa and I finally get some much-needed sleep. Tomorrow I have a date with Brazil.

we are nippon

15

Tickets, Any Tickets?

At matches in Japan on June 1 and 2 there were 237,000 empty seats. The Japan organising committee, JAWOC, learned that Byrom, the UK-based company responsible for ticket sales outside of Japan, still held some tickets. Byrom claimed they didn't. Ticket demand in Japan was hugely oversubscribed and millions of people were left disappointed.

At Saitama Stadium for the Japan vs. Belgium game, many fans were left outside the ground, appealing for tickets and yet unable to afford the prices that touts demanded. Interviewed by television, the fans complained bitterly.

'Why don't they just let us in? I want to support Japan.'

'Look, there are hundreds of empty seats. It's ridiculous!'

The television cameras zoomed in over the stand to show row upon row of empty seats in the main stand.

A huge row began as JAWOC claimed that Byrom were selling tickets on match days for games they had previously said were sold out. JAWOC also claimed they could not get overseas sales data from Byrom, as under the ticket sale agreement, JAWOC had no right to interfere with overseas sales.

JAWOC decided to reverse its previous policy and began selling tickets on match days. Byrom refused to give any information to JAWOC, who in turn claimed that this was so Byrom could hold on to tickets for as long as possible, in order to maximize their own profits. Under the ticketing agreement, Byrom took a 9% commission from each ticket they sold, a commission they would have lost if they had returned tickets to JAWOC.

Byrom is a UK-based firm run by three Mexican brothers, including Jaime Byrom, who has connections with Sepp Blatter. Byrom was also responsible for players' and officials' accommodation, as they were at USA 94. Before the 2002 World Cup, Byrom had no experience of printing or selling tickets.

On June 6, JAWOC announced the sale of 40,000 tickets via the Internet and by telephone. Byrom said that all their work in processing tickets was done and anyone with any questions should go to FIFA. A JAWOC staffer said that they were receiving calls from the public, who had been re-directed to them by FIFA. Byrom and FIFA officials were seen enjoying World Cup games together in Japan.

About 700,000 tickets for games in Japan, half the total number, were allocated for sale overseas. Of these, 30% went to the general public, 40% to international football associations and 30% to sponsors. As the public allocation was said to be sold, the sponsors and FA tickets were said to be the root of the problem. Some claimed only 50-60% of this allocation was taken up.

In a measure to counter hooliganism and prevent fraud, tickets sold to the public had the name of the purchaser printed on them and there were to be name checks at the gate. The sponsors' tickets, however, had no name printed on them. Perhaps because sponsors and their guests are intrinsically trustworthy, or perhaps so that, if any unused tickets ended up being passed onto touts or troublemakers, they couldn't be traced back to the sponsor.

International FAs were also involved in profiteering. The Nigerian FA sold tickets for the England game in Osaka for five times the face value and at Wing Stadium in Kobe, some Belgians I spoke to had bought their tickets directly from the Belgian FA at face value, plus a 10% 'administration fee'.

Whatever the ins and outs of the bickering between Byrom, FIFA and JAWOC, the ordinary fans are the ones that always lose out. Touts claimed business was slow except for games involving Japan, England, Italy and Argentina. Tickets for Japan vs. Belgium were said to be selling for up to ¥200,000 (£1,080), and over that for Japan vs. Russia. The biggest price reportedly paid for a ticket to see Japan play Belgium was ¥600,000 (£3,240), for a VIP seat at a game where around 7,000 seats were empty.

In the event, there were no name checks at the gates. It had been calculated that checking every ticket would take around seven hours. A JAWOC official said the event was an international football festival and, well, what could be done?

A few days before the tournament kicked-off, 100,000 tickets had still not arrived from Byrom, who claimed the confusion of the two languages, cultures and unfamiliar fonts needed for printing had caused the delays.

A storm of frustration arose and one fan trying to buy Japan vs. Russia tickets at a distribution centre was arrested after he fought with officials and security guards, pushing an official through a glass door. The fan was frustrated by the complicated buying process. Fans were told to phone JAWOC first to get a reference number. They should then pay the money into the JAWOC account at a convenience store, after which they could collect their tickets from a designated ticket centre. If the fan happened to live in Ibaraki or Sapporo, they would have to travel a considerable distance, as there were no distribution centres in those host cities.

A new phrase that entered the lexicon during the World Cup was 'seat kills'. The term described seats deemed unfit for sale, as they had a restricted view. At the Japan vs. Turkey game in Miyagi, 700 seat kills were mistakenly made in the main stand opposite the team benches. The Miyagi governor said he would consider legal action against Byrom. The national government joined in and said Byrom had ignored people's feelings and was 'impotent and irresponsible'.

FIFA jumped to Byrom's defence, making an official statement to the media via their website. The statement claimed there were inappropriate seat kills because JAWOC had failed to identify an error in the stadium seating plan. Responsibility, FIFA said, had to be shared. In an extraordinary defence of Byrom, the statement went on to say Byrom had rescued the ticketing process from a crisis situation. The crisis was due to the late receipt of information from JAWOC. This meant, the statement went on, that Byrom had to do six months' work in six weeks and it was only thanks to their innovative system by which smart cards and credit cards were converted to tickets, that thousands of fans could easily obtain tickets.

In the second week of the tournament, Byrom was revealed to have cancelled 25,000 reservations at hotels throughout Japan. They refused to pay the 100% cancellation fees. At a conservative estimate of ¥10,000 (£54) per room per night, that means an unpaid promise of ¥250 million (£1.35 million).

FIFA, despite its protestations that JAWOC should do the same, would shoulder no responsibility for the actions of the company.

Some people did benefit from the fiasco, however. The Russia vs. Tunisia game at Wing Stadium was around 11,000 below capacity. The local government in Shizuoka, the site of the Russian training camp, gave away 780 tickets to local school children.

we are nippon

16

The Boys from Brazil – Brazil vs. Belgium

In the group stages of the tournament in Japan, aside from the home team, England has enjoyed unparalleled backing from the home nation. Every England game has been like a home game, perhaps even better. England's popularity in Japan is huge, unrivalled.

The only team that could come anywhere near threatening that support is a potential champion, plays in yellow and has just arrived from Korea. For Brazil, Japan is a home away from home.

At the beginning of the 20th century, as Japanese natural resources were scarce, the government began advising its population to emigrate. The open spaces of South America were seen as an ideal destination, and people began leaving for plots of land in Brazil and Peru. Some also made their way to North America and Hawaii. The result of this mass migration is that Brazil now has a population of around one million ethnic Japanese.

In the 'bubble' years of the late 1980s, the Japanese economy expanded rapidly and looked set for world domination. At the lower end of the wage scale, there was a labour shortage as the population again turned its backs on 3-K manual labour. A country that is notoriously opposed to immigration faced a dilemma, an influx of workers was needed, but Asian immigrants were seen as undesirable. Thus, in 1989, the immigration laws were changed to allow second- and third-generation Japanese to work in Japan, the assumption being that they would be familiar with the Japanese language, way of life and culture. There was an influx of people from Brazil seeking a better standard of living and of the 1.7 million foreigners living in Japan (about 1.4% of the total population), Brazilians are now the third-largest group, following those from the Koreas and China.

In football, too, Japan and Brazil are inextricably linked. Since the J.League started in 1993, dozens of Brazilians have played in Japan, including several of the squad that won USA 94. Though recently, because of satellite television and the increasing popularity of stars such as Beckham and Owen, English football is popular, it is against Brazil that Japan wish to match themselves.

When Brazil arrive from their group stage in Korea, they are greeted by a huge crowd and fêted in a way that befits the four-time world champions.

For the game at Wing Stadium in Kobe, a large crowd of Brazilians,

Brazilian-Japanese and Japanese-Brazil fans is present to cheer on the South American superstars.

Aleyne Egashira, an ethnic Japanese born in São Paolo, who has lived in Japan since she was eight, has slightly mixed allegiances.

'I support Japan, but not against Brazil.'

Though we speak to each other in Japanese, Aleyne displays the pride in the country of her first name from top to toe. She is wearing a Brazil headband, a black vest with the Brazil flag inside a green heart and cotton trousers ablaze with green, yellow and blue flowers in the style of the flag.

Another fan, Japanese born and bred, but a fan of Brazil since he started playing football 20 years ago, ten years before the J.League started, says things are a little more complicated.

'If Japan play Brazil, I won't know who to support. Maybe I'd support Japan in the first half and Brazil in the second.'

A hat-seller from Argentina I met in Sapporo is wearing the yellow of her traditional rivals.

'Of course I want them to win, because now they represent the hopes of all of South America.'

I wonder if I could choose who I would want to lose more if Argentina played Germany.

The World Cup does strange things to people. It unites some nations against others and gives people a temporary adopted nationality. There is, though, one country everyone wants to lose. In the media centre watching the last 30 minutes of Mexico vs. the USA, the USA are that team. The packed media centre has English, Italians, Brazilians and French all supporting Mexico. There are two American journalists, who, even if they weren't whooping, would be easily spotted. They wear their country's uniform polo shirt tucked into beige chinos hanging above tan deck shoes.

The score is USA 1, Mexico 0.

As I find a seat, a Mexican penalty appeal is turned down to much exhaling to my right and some whooping behind me. Mexico have lots of possession and look like they'll equalise.

Then, the USA strike on the break and Landon Donovan scores with a header. There is more whooping behind me and multi-lingual swearing to my right. Mexican heads drop and they lose their way, resorting to hacking and kicking. Everyone in the media centre, except the two Americans, is pleased to see Cobi Jones felled. In a show of unmitigated bias, we yell at the referee when he shows Rafael Marquez a red card.

'What was that for?'

The Americans win. Annoyed, I troop off.

Inside, the stadium is awash with yellow and the samba band is making its Japanese debut. There are samba bands in the J.League, but this is the real thing. The crowd are mostly Japanese, but they are lapping it up, dancing in front of their seats. These cannot be the same people, surely, who two days ago got excited by the conga and 'We're Not Going Home'.

A Mexican wave goes round the stadium three times before kick-off – everyone joins in. There is a fantastic, upbeat atmosphere. The carnival has come to Kobe.

For all the support Brazil have, Belgium make a good fist of spoiling the party and they have a shot tipped over the bar inside the first five minutes. The samba is undaunted, though, and when Robert Carlos takes a corner, the number of flashes rivals that for Beckham. People prefer to take the moment home to watch over and over again, than to see it in the flesh.

A Rivaldo bicycle-kick attempt gets a huge cheer, as the stars of Brazil play to the cameras. When Marc Wilmots does the same thing a few moments later, the cheers are even louder and seem to come from a section of bright yellow.

This inspires Belgium to get a chant going, which, like England's, is monotonous and lacks rhythm. Their team, though, are playing well, they pack their midfield and stifle Brazil, causing them problems going forward. After 36 minutes, the crowd are momentarily silenced as Wilmots heads home, only to have his effort harshly ruled out for a push.

At half-time, two Belgians in headbands tell me that the referee is in FIFA's back pocket and disallowed the goal to keep Brazil in the tournament, 'just like last time'.

In the queue for drinks the fans have elbows a photographer would be proud of and when I get to the front, the only things left to eat are cold noodles for ¥450.

In the second half, Belgium take the game to Brazil, Wilmots going close twice in ten minutes. Marcos in the Brazil goal saves his team twice and then a third time before Ronaldinho, against the run of play, passes to Rivaldo who controls with his chest and hits a magnificent volley, his whole body parallel to the ground. His brilliance is exaggerated by a deflection off a defender that takes the ball out of Geert de Vlieger's reach, but the crowd don't care and they raise the roof. The samba begins with energy anew as Brazil perform in the style they are supposed to.

Brazil settle down after the goal, keeping possession, while the Belgians seem to run out of steam. Three minutes from the end, Kleberson feeds Ronaldo from the right, who stabs it home, making him the tournament's joint-top scorer, as he begins to look like his old self.

After the game, the Brazil players in the media mixed zone say they couldn't believe the support, that it had won them the game and they hoped that it would continue in their next game.

That game is against England. Beckham and the rest of the England squad had watched the game from the VIP seats in Wing Stadium. They caused a commotion when they arrived, people turning to watch them sit down. When they left early to avoid the crush, nobody in the stands in front of them watched Brazil. Everybody turned around to watch Beckham and England make their exit, cheering them as they left. People in the stand either side turned and craned their necks and people looked down from the stand above. Perhaps England, in the stands at least, may just have the edge in six days' time.

Outside, the samba band samba to the station. The woman at the front wears a bikini and feathered headdress, the man playing guitar wears a fez, behind him the drummer wears a vest and headdress and at the back, a fat man without an instrument wears a tight yellow body suit and a green wig. They are a happy, colourful procession and everyone wants to join in. Across the street a young woman shows off her toenails, painted with the flags of ten competing countries. A man has a green cardboard box on his head, his painted blue face sticking out to form a Brazil flag. Three red devils are talking to a Japanese-Brazilian couple, Roberto and Terumi. Terumi is wearing a yellow bikini top. She poses for a photograph with two of the Belgians, her Brazilian blood getting the better of her Japanese as she drops her bikini top to reveal her breasts. Despite many requests, there is no repeat performance.

Television crews follow the samba band onto the subway. Everyone waits patiently as the police hold the crowd back and let them down into the subway in groups to avoid a crush.

The samba band gets onto the train as the carnival pulls out of Kobe. Next stop Shizuoka and England.

17

Troussier Nippon

One of the more memorable chants of the 2002 World Cup could be heard all over Japan.

'Troussier Nippon!'

It was accompanied by five sharp claps of the hands.

'Troussier Nippon!'

The chant was sung from the stadium seats.

'Troussier Nippon!'

It was sung wherever Japanese fans gathered.

'Troussier Nippon!'

It was sung at Saitama.

'Troussier Nippon!'

Shibuya.

'Troussier Nippon!'

Yokohama.

'Troussier Nippon!'

Roppongi.

'Troussier Nippon!'

Osaka.

'Troussier Nippon!'

Ebisu Bridge.

'Troussier Nippon!'

It was sung to celebrate victory.

'Troussier Nippon!'

It was sung to commemorate defeat.

'Troussier Nippon!'

It seemed to punctuate every minute of the 2002 World Cup.

'Troussier Nippon!'

It was even sung at the airport when Troussier left Japan for the last time and flew home to France in mid-July.

'Troussier Nippon!'

That the Japanese fans were singing their team coach, Philippe Troussier's name at all marked something of a turnaround.

In France 98, Japan went further than they had ever gone by qualifying for the World Cup finals. Under manager Okada Takeshi, they scored one goal, but lost all of their games. Okada had no previous coaching experience and was a last ditch appointment.

Okada did well under the intense media spotlight that accompanied Japan's first World Cup adventure, but after the tournament, he was keen to shun the limelight and resigned, later to become the manager of J.League minnows Consadole Sapporo.

Okada looked like a typical Japanese salaryman in glasses, grey suit and non-descript, pudding-bowl haircut. He seemed out of place in charge of a group of wealthy young professionals, including the outspoken, self-confident Nakata Hidetoshi and other fashionable, young media-darlings with dyed hair, designer clothes and model girlfriends.

When the Japan Football Association began a search for Okada's successor, they looked abroad to bring in some foreign expertise. A shortlist of desired coaches was drawn up, and at the top of the list was the name, Philippe Troussier.

Troussier came with an impressive CV that included club and national team successes. Whilst in Africa he had been given the name the 'White Witch Doctor' and had earned something of a reputation. He was said to be aggressive, surly and had a terrible relationship with the media, whom he despised. The feeling was mutual and a cartoon by South African political cartoonist Jonathan Shapiro showed Troussier biting the head off a journalist and spitting out the bloody remnants. When he arrived in Japan, Troussier didn't speak any Japanese and by the time he departed, nothing had changed.

Troussier was the famed journeyman of French football. He got his first professional contract as a player in 1975. When he retired in 1983, he had hardly set the world alight. He became a qualified masseur and physiotherapist and took a master's degree in sports science. As a self-proclaimed intellectual, he was regarded suspiciously by his fellow professionals.

In 1989, ever the renegade, Troussier moved to the Ivory Coast in Africa, where he managed ASEC Abidjan, leading them to three consecutive league titles. Inspired by this success, the Ivory Coast FA appointed him manager of the national team in 1993. He subsequently moved on to South Africa and then Morocco. His seven months at the helm in Nigeria between March and September in1997 saw them secure a place at France 98. It was during this period that his nickname was coined.

Troussier then moved on to Burkina Faso, pulling the national team up by its bootstraps to the dizzy heights of fourth place in the African Nations Cup on home turf in 1998. He fell out with the football authorities and moved on again, becoming South Africa coach once more for France 98. This time success eluded him. Stubborn with players he couldn't convince of his viewpoint, Troussier was roundly criticized by the media.

Just as it seemed his star was fading, Troussier was offered *carte blanche* by the JFA to reshape and prepare them for the World Cup four years later. Troussier, ever relishing a challenge, jumped at the chance and took control of the youth, under-21 and full sides, determined to toughen them up physically and mentally in an attempt to take on the world's best.

Troussier had noted that though the Japanese were skillful, they were lacking in the physical aspects of the game, something he thought was the result of an inferiority complex. He invited a sports analyst from Dijon University to do some tests. The tests proved that the Japanese had stronger muscles than Europeans, but that strength didn't translate into speed. After analysing the games that the Japanese played, he noticed there was little in the way of shirt-pulling, sliding-tackles or elbowing. Troussier then set about teaching his players how to do these things, demonstrating the techniques himself. This physical approach led him to be dubbed 'Green Beret' by sections of the media.

Troussier identified this lack of speed and physical bite, along with a lack of international experience at either club or national level, as the first things he had to change. He also noticed that the older, more experienced players received too much respect. The younger players, no matter their ability, looked up too much to their supposed betters.

Respect for seniority is a Confucian value the Japanese adopted from China. It is present in Japanese when speaking deferentially to one's perceived inferiors. Juniors address their seniors as *sempai*. The seniors in turn follow their juniors' names with the address *kun*, as would an adult a child.

This is a habit adhered to at sports clubs in schools, where team members are expected to practice every day, including weekends and holidays. Their devotion to the cause is absolute. On weekends taking the subway into town, I often see sports teams on their way home after a match or practice. The senior members sit on the seats, the junior members on the floor at the end of the carriage. When a senior member gets up to get off the train, the junior members stand, bow and say, '*Otsukare sama desu* – thank you for your hard work.'

Troussier identified Nakata Hidetoshi, by now a star with Roma in Serie A, as a problem. Although he could inspire the team, Troussier felt he had a negative effect on others, making them awestruck and nervous. Troussier also bristled at Nakata's strong streak of individualism, which he felt made him an unsuitable leader.

Troussier felt that he had to make the team one big family, where everyone was respected for their ability, not their age or assumed rank.

Troussier attacked the media, saying they knew nothing about football, and didn't try to educate the Japanese public about it, concentrating only on the celebrities of the team and looking for gossip. Aside from 'Green Beret', Troussier was labelled 'gay' and 'Red Devil' for his short temper.

In April 2000, Japan lost to Korea in Seoul and Troussier was vilified by the media. His contract was up for renewal that June and much of the press had decided that he would be replaced. Troussier didn't help his own image by appearing arrogant and aloof, though negotiating with the Japanese FA, renowned for their difficult internal politics, can have been no easy thing.

In October 2000, with Troussier's hand still on the tiller, Japan won the Asia Cup and his methods were seen to have been proven. He had made the team more combative, made his players learn more than one position and now said they should go abroad to learn more than they could in the J.League.

In 2001, the Confederations Cup in Japan was seen as a dry run for the World Cup. While there were some notable gaffes off the field, the Japanese team made it to the final by beating an Australian team physically their superiors. The Japanese challenged and slid in as never before, earning a place in the final against then world and European champions, France. Japan had lost to France 5-0 a few months earlier. This time, in a creditable performance against a strong French side, they lost 1-0.

The world's most famous Japanese player, Nakata Hidetoshi, was absent. He had flown back to Italy for Roma's last game of the season, widening the rift between him and Troussier.

With no qualifying games to play, Troussier said he had no time for prima donnas and led Japan, minus Nakata, in 13 friendlies, beating Yugoslavia, Cameroon and Paraguay and drawing with Brazil, Nigeria and Italy.

The team was stronger, more confident and played a quick, short passing game. Troussier made overtures to Nakata and before the World Cup said that Japan were capable of winning the tournament. A poll of fans showed 80% thought they had a chance of winning. In four years, Troussier had turned the footballing nation around.

He still had a trick up his sleeve, though. When he named his World Cup squad, Nakamura Shunsuke's name was not on the list. Nakamura was Japan's newest superstar with a domestic following to rival Nakata. He excelled at free-kicks and his creativity in open play had linked him with a move to Real Madrid. He later moved to Italian Serie A side Reggina.

Nakamura, though gifted on the pitch, was not particularly skilled when dealing with the media and on camera was often surly. In one interview he said that he never had a clue what Troussier was talking about. Troussier claimed that Nakamura and Nakata could not play together and that Nakamura was too small and too easily dispossessed.

Though he says he used mind games and silence to communicate with his players and make them think, Troussier is perhaps not the philosopher he claims to be. He is though, well aware of the impact of metaphor.

In his book, *Passion*, Troussier talks of speaking sternly to the players before a game, like he is a matador thrusting a banderilla into a bull. He deliberately sets the lighting low in a room when speaking and chooses his clothes carefully for each match, depending on the conditions and the opponent.

Nor is he afraid of nationalism or patriotism. He says when he hears 'Kimigayo', tears well up in his eyes and he prays for the ancestors of Japan. He says he becomes a member of the Japanese family at this time of national unity and that the country's history crystallises itself in a single moment. He says that, because of his age, he feels this more than his players as he is closer to the symbolism associated with war.

He notes that the players in the tunnel look straight ahead as before a battle.

'Troussier Nippon!'
'Troussier Nippon!'
'Troussier Nippon!'

we are nippon

18

The Middle of Nowhere – Japan vs. Turkey

Having only got to bed at 3 a.m., and waking a mere three hours later, I am exhausted again and still mumbling to myself that this has to stop, this whirl of travelling, football, drinking and dancing. This international festival is taking its toll.

I get the 7.33 Shinkansen, or bullet train, from Shin-Osaka Station. Unable to make a seat reservation with the ticket I have and given that the train is not starting from Osaka, but has come from Okayama, 113 miles away, it's already packed when it arrives. I am late to get to the platform and there are already long queues. By the time I get on the train, all the available seats have been taken and I have to sit on the floor in the spaces between the carriages again, this time next to the toilet. I have a brief look up and down the train for empty seats. There are none. I almost choke to death when passing through the fug in the smoking section as hundreds of smokers puff their way to important business in East Japan. I smell of smoke for the rest of the day.

When I finally get a seat at Nagoya, around an hour into the journey, I'm joined by a Japanese football fan wearing his country's colours who, at 8.30 in the morning, has a can of beer in his hand. Internationalisation has worn me out, left me short of sleep and hung over. When he stretches out the hand of international friendship, I slap it back.

'*Gu-do morningu*! Where do you come from?'

'Ugh. England.' I grunt back, as un-internationally as I can, which I manage very well.

'Oh, *Ingurando?*' He intones downwards, disappointed.

I take out my notebook and pretend to write, feeling guilty. My would-be friend closes his eyes and pretends to sleep.

Twenty minutes later he is haranguing the train conductor as to why he couldn't get the information he needed about trains connecting from Tokyo to Miyagi when he rang JR West last night. The conductor replies that as there are two companies, JR East and JR West, neither has the timetables of the other. Unsatisfied with this answer and possibly fuelled by his early morning lager, my travelling companion pursues a strident line of moaning and complaining. From his accent he is obviously from Osaka, and he is a stereotypical Osakan at that – loud and obnoxious. I did the right thing, I content myself, by ignoring him.

Fifteen minutes later, he's at the conductor again, asking about connecting trains from Tokyo, waving his timetable about and making an awful racket. I can't bear it. I blow my cover, telling him there is a connecting train from Tokyo at 11.04. They both look at me and the conductor carries on down the train. I realise my mistake as I am complimented on my Japanese. I grunt again and do my best to get out of the conversation as quickly as possible, steadfastly refusing to look him in the face, then taking my turn to pretend to sleep.

On arriving at the platform before departure I was sweating heavily, though the sky was dark and heavy with the promise of rain. Since the train left Osaka, the rain has been pelting down and visibility is severely reduced in a misty fog. Miyagi will be wet, chilly and humid – awful conditions for football, whether playing or watching.

Changing at Tokyo for the Tohoku Line, after another hour, the weather has cleared sufficiently for visibility to have returned to more than ten yards. We wend our way through two-storeyed suburbia, the odd, tall chimney, marking out a *sento* – a public bath-house – towering above the houses.

All the houses look alike, a muddy grey colour with steel-grey roofs. They are typical of the new style of housing slowly replacing the older – the post-war kind with off-white walls and heavy, curved, ceramic tiles in green or blue. These postwar buildings had themselves replaced the old wooden houses, whose extremities were charred to prevent the spread of fire. A major advantage of the new type of housing that stands along the Tohoku Line is that the roofs are light and the sections of the house are connected by high-tension wire. This allows them to rock with any earthquakes that might happen, stopping the roof from caving in and killing those inside. They don't look half as nice, though.

Two rows in front of me, a screaming child is ordering his parents around, telling them he doesn't want to sit here, he wants to sit there, that he doesn't want to do this, he wants to do that. The parents indulge the little monster for about 30 minutes, though this doesn't stop his screaming. I'm about to either tell them to do something about it, tell him to shut up or just reach forward and strangle the little brat when we thankfully pull into Sendai. I am relieved to get off.

The public train network in Japan is fantastic and makes travel easy, though it does mean that the public have to be dealt with. This very often is not easy. Old men make clicking noises with their tongues, cleaning the insides of their mouths. Others chew gum with their mouths wide open, doing passable impressions of goats. Young women primp and preen themselves, applying their make-up, which they check in mirrors they unfold from their bags. Men sniff, snort and cough up phlegm, all perfectly acceptable behaviour where the production of a handkerchief would astound. On the subway line in Osaka, I once saw a child biting his toenails.

On the media shuttle bus to the stadium, I sit next to a man who reeks of cigarette smoke. Whilst thinking he must have come all the way from Osaka in the smoking carriage, I realise the smell is coming from a portable ashtray he is wearing on a cord around his neck. He may well have bought this as part of the 'Smokin' Clean' campaign. This urges smokers to take just such portable ashtrays with them into the countryside when hiking or fishing, not to discard their butts on the street and pay attention to no-smoking signs. Japan is a smokers' paradise. Public places that are unsupervised, and therefore not cleaned, are usually littered with cigarette ends and no-smoking areas are blithely ignored.

Miyagi Stadium is in the middle of nowhere – a concrete monument to the backhanders and pork-barrel politics Shintani had explained on the train to Niigata. Driving the 40-minute ride from Sendai Station, the money the LDP must have received from this faceless suburbia mounts up with every yard. We trundle on concrete roads through a housing estate that looks like countless, faceless, tasteless Barrett or Wimpy estates in the middle of nowhere in the middle of England.

The estate ends and the bus crosses a concrete bridge over a rare sight: a river in its natural state. Native, green forest stretches to the banks of the river, where it dips its fingers in the water. The banks are lined with long grass, rather than the concrete walls that have replaced nature along the banks of most of Japan's rivers. Around 3,000 concrete dams have been built since the 1960s, often in the most remote of places across the narrowest of streams. The concrete lines the river banks and the coffers of the LDP in a country with a rainfall of twice the global average.

I get to the media centre and pick up my ticket for the pitch and promptly ask the group of photographers on the waiting list if anyone would like to swap.

My ticket is snapped up by a photographer whose colleague says I told you so.

'See, I told you, you'll always get a ticket for outside when it's raining, there's always someone who doesn't want to be out in the rain.'

'I'm English and the rain doesn't bother me,' I say, 'I just thought the ticket might be more use to someone else.'

'Oh. Sorry for being rude. Do you live in Osaka?'

Elsewhere in the media centre, an Australian writer tells me that he has heard a rumour that FIFA have told the referees for today's games to make sure that both host countries get through to the next round. Imagine, he says, if Japan and Korea have to play in Seoul for third place.

Imagine. War.

Walking out from the media centre to the stadium is the most bizarre walk imaginable. Miyagi Stadium truly is in the middle of nowhere. Access to the stands is over a field, over a footbridge that crosses a wide path and then up a sharp grassy incline. The approach is more Stonehenge than Wembley Way. Aside from the stadium and the adjoining running track, all that can be seen for miles around are pylons that stand on the top of green hills. Security guards wearing thin shirts use short plastic batons to guide people along a footpath. The batons have a strip light inside them that shines in the rainy season gloom, doubly effective on a path that only goes in one direction.

A long concrete path winds around the stadium to the media tribune.

The weather is foul. The rainy season is offering its worst and the normally bright blue shirts in the stands are darkened somewhat by the transparent raingear given out free at the entrances. The day is overcast and the stadium floodlights are on at 3 p.m. in the afternoon. Those in the ends behind the goals who aren't wearing raingear are drenched.

Opposite the main stand there are blocks of empty seats.

The weather dampens the atmosphere a little, but once the voice screams into the megaphone, the crowd comes alive.

'Ni–*pp*on! Ni–*pp*on! Ni–*pp*on!'

During 'Kimigayo', Nakata's face briefly appears on screen through the red of the Hinomaru. The royal prince and princess are here. This could be the biggest day in the nation's short footballing history.

After kick-off, Japan look out of sorts. Troussier has changed a so-far winning formula and introduced Alex and Nishizawa from the start. Alex doesn't seem to know where to play and his team-mates seem equally lost. He drifts out to the left and gets in the way of Ono, then back inside and gets in the way of Nakata.

The crowd boo every Turkish touch, but on 12 minutes, when Turkey score with a header from a poorly defended corner, the stadium falls silent. The defenders look at each other, as if to ask who was supposed to be marking whom. Nobody was marking anybody. It's a cheap goal to concede and not like the Japan of the first three games.

Nishizawa, who plays for Cerezo in the second division of a second-rate J.League, is lost alone up front. Unable to get a game for Bolton during a brief spell on loan in England, Nishizawa was sent back to Osaka, where he has since been equally unsuccessful. Troussier is playing true to form and has surprised everyone.

Hopeful crosses from the wings have no chance of being converted and though Japan keep pressing, the Turks defend comfortably. In the last few minutes of the half, Alex hits a free-kick onto the bar and Ozalan Alpay heads narrowly over his own goal.

For the second half, Troussier makes another strange decision. He leaves Nishizawa on, but brings off Alex and Inamoto, Japan's top-scorer, to replace them with Suzuki and Ichikawa. Troussier seems to have his halves the wrong way round.

Japan dominate midfield, but their final ball is poor and they give it away too easily. This is the Japan of before the World Cup. Something has happened, something is different. The fight that was shown in the first three games just isn't there. Perhaps they are tired, perhaps it's the weather, perhaps Troussier has said something to them.

Troussier, animated at all Japan's games so far, sits slumped on the bench, his chin on his hand. Silent, his interpreter has nothing to do.

The Turkish defence have little to do either, as Japan create nothing and Turkey keep them at bay until the end.

The final, defeating whistle is greeted with a stony silence. The Turks show they have learnt their manners and run to each side of the pitch, linking hands and bowing to all sides of the crowd, just as Japanese teams do. They receive generous applause.

The crowd keep up the chants of 'Troussier Nippon', and as the team and management do a lap of honour, the crowd applauds them as heroes. As they continue, they have to compete for the crowd's attention with a loud advert blasting from the giant screen.

Troussier tries to console his players, but they are dejected. Still popular with the crowd and having finally won the media over, there is still some resentment against Troussier amongst the players. Toda will later say that he never wants to set eyes on Troussier again.

Troussier turns to all sides of the stadium and waves before disappearing down the tunnel for the last time as manager. Interviewed after the game, he says he is proud of his team and that they have come a long way in four years. He calls it the end of an adventure. It's more of a rainy season damp squib.

The fans outside show some disappointment, but not too much. Nobody calls Troussier names, but a few question his tactics. Everyone puts a brave face on things.

'We did well to get this far.'

'*Zannen* – It's a shame.'

'They did their best.'

'I thought they'd win, but, well, never mind.'

'*Sho ga nai* – It can't be helped.'

This is typical Japanese fortitude. This is also shown by one of the illuminated-baton-equipped security guards. As I cross over the footbridge, away from Stonehenge and back to the media centre, he raises his baton with his left hand and ushers me across the bridge. There is no other way I could go. He is soaked to the skin, shivering and his teeth are chattering.

'How long have you been standing there?'

'Since one o'clock.'

It is now after six.

I cross over the bridge and outside the door to the media centre I find a disposed-of disposable umbrella. I pick it up and take it back across the footbridge and try to hand it to the security guard. Speaking English, he refuses.

'No! No!'

Repeating the journey in reverse back to the station, I am thoroughly depressed. Japan should have won the game, but the dream is over. This time the grey suburbia looks even worse. These are the boring houses and the boring, repetitive lives that people will return to now the excitement of Japan's World Cup run has gone.

At Sendai Station I have time to grab something to eat before catching the train back to Tokyo. I go to Lotteria, a fast-food restaurant. Lotteria are not one of the sponsors of the World Cup and therefore do not have any World Cup-related merchandise, songs or promotions. I choose a *yaki bibimba* set from the menu. *Yaki bibimba* is a popular Korean dish of rice, vegetables, mince, *kimchi* and a potent chili sauce, mixed together in pre-heated stone bowls. The Lotteria *yaki bibimba* set, however, makes buns of the rice and has the other ingredients sealed together in a fried – perhaps poached, I can't be exactly sure – egg. There are far too many options available to complete my set. I have to choose the size of my drink – small, medium or large; its temperature – hot or cold – the size of my chips and which sauce I'd like to accompany them: tomato, mayonnaise or butter and soy sauce. I choose the last and after paying, I'm asked politely to wait by the girl who is serving me.

She is wearing a Pepsi T-shirt, which says on the front, 'Ask for more.' I'm severely tempted, but keep my mouth closed. Her back is turned for a couple of seconds while she retrieves my chips from the racks behind her.

'Just a few more moments, please.'

She turns away again, then back to me and has my coffee on the tray in a jiffy.

'Please wait just a little longer.'

She turns away again and then turns back, my *yaki bibimba* burger completing the set. The whole process has taken less than a minute.

'I'm awfully sorry to have kept you waiting for so long. Please relax and enjoy your meal.'

I ignore her advice, difficult anyway in a crowded restaurant with bored people looking for someone to stare at, and wolf down the *yaki bibimba* set as quickly as I can. I am soon upstairs and on the platform, ten minutes before my train leaves.

The platform is crowded and people are chattering away in the strange accents of this part of the country. I move to the front of the platform. There is always more space there, most people not being able to sum up the energy to walk the extra few yards from the top of the steps.

The queue is 30-40 people long and there is no chance of getting a seat – perhaps only a slim chance of actually getting on the train.

A man in the queue is drinking a can of beer and suddenly I'm desperate for a drink. I ask him to watch my bags while I go back down the platform to the kiosk where they sell *bento* (lunch boxes), sandwiches, snacks and beer; I buy three cans of Kirin Ichiban Shibori – Kirin First Squeeze.

I get back to the queue and my bags are there, diligently being watched. The train pulls in and I realise that it is not coming to us. The queues are staggered in threes down the platform and alternate trains stop with their doors at different spots, allowing people to queue for three different trains at the same time. More remarkable is that the trains are timetabled to arrive on time at such frequency and stop at different positions on the platform. The train arrives on time and stops at the required spot. Shinkansen trains that are late are known to make the evening television news.

The beginning of each queue is marked by a different shape on the platform and the train is listed next to the corresponding shape on the electronic departure board. A superb example of well-thought-out, simple rules, which, when adhered to, make things easy for everyone. I can't quite picture the Argentinian hat-seller, Macedonian journalist or the Brazilian-Japanese bikini-dropper adhering to the rules, though. In England, people would have to wait all day for trains that never arrived.

One-third of the queue I'm standing in realise that they are in the wrong place and make a mad dash for another queue they will be at the end of. They will get to Tokyo 25 minutes earlier, but I doubt they'll get a seat. Two hours standing does not appeal. My chances of getting a seat have just significantly improved by not moving. I stay where I am.

The train I wait for doesn't get in to Tokyo until 10.20 p.m., meaning I'll miss the Korea vs. Italy game. I phone Pak and Kumai and they both promise to keep me informed via email to my phone.

The train pulls in and we all pile on, making a dash for the few empty seats. No one makes way for anyone else. A young lad in front of me goes past one empty seat, presumably looking for a better one or one he can sit in with his friend. He realises his mistake and that he has just gone past the last free seat in the carriage. Just as my backside is about to hit the seat, he tries to place his *bento* on it to reserve it. He scoops his *bento* away just in time to stop it being crushed, thus surrendering the seat to me. I feel no need to apologise for this inevitability and, inordinately happy, I crack open a can of First Squeeze to celebrate.

My feelings of well-being are disturbed soon after departure by a couple in their late 40s. They have come from further down the train in search of seats and realise there are none. They sit on the floor in the aisle next to my seat, their chins on their chests as they try to sleep. They look terribly uncomfortable. In a not-often-seen show of affection between man and woman, particularly middle-aged, married ones, they hold hands as their heads bob with the rhythm of the train. I do my best to ignore them, but by the last drop of the First Squeeze, my manners have got the better of me and I get up and offer my seat to the woman.

She of course refuses.

'No, no, it's quite alright.'

'No, I insist.'

'No, really, it's OK.'

'I've been sitting there for a while, and I insist you take it. I'm going to sit on the floor, so you might as well.'

I sit on the floor.

'Well, if you're quite sure. Thank you very much.'

I had intended that the woman could sleep, but now I'm embroiled in a conversation with her and her husband, who plies me with beer and Kit-Kats. We discuss Troussier's selection, my Osaka accent and the amazing crowds in Korea. The husband displays mixed feelings.

'I don't want Korea to do badly, but I don't want them to do better than Japan. It won't be good for international relations if they do better than us. Normally, I would want the Asian team to do well. It's tricky. I don't want to say "I hope Italy beat them" but, well, Italy are a strong European side...'

They get off before Tokyo, giving me the seat back for the last 40 minutes of the journey.

I try to call Pak, but I can't get through and I realise I don't have his phone's email address. I email Kumai who replies straight back saying that Italy are beating Korea 1-0. This is perfect, just as Pak had wanted before the tournament started. Japan and Korea both do well, but fail at the same point in the tournament; at the same stage, with the same number of wins, draws and losses. Perfect symmetry. Perfect for the internationalists. My mood improves significantly.

The train arrives in Tokyo and I get off, feeling the effect of the cans I bought and those I was given. I decide to go to Shibuya to see if any crowds have gathered there and make my way over to the Yamanote Line. Riding the train in a circle around the capital, happily tipsy, I am friendly to any- and everyone, asking people if they know the score in the Korea game. Everyone ignores me and I feel like I'm a stranger arriving in London, taking the Tube for the first time. One woman then looks up and says that the score was 1-0 to Italy last she heard.

Bored with the carriage I'm in, I walk down into the next, looking for someone to talk to, to continue the spirit of inebriated internationalism. Before I can latch onto some hapless victim, my phone buzzes and vibrates in my pocket, chirruping away in a perfect digital imitation of a cicada, the delightful function my phone has to tell me an email has arrived.

It's from Kumai.

'Korea equalized in the last minute and are in Golden Goals.'

This is bad news.

Great for Korea, great for football, but this means that Korea, even if they lose, have progressed further than Japan. This will not go down well.

I walk back through to the other carriage and tell the woman who spoke to me that Korea have equalized.

'You're kidding? Oh no!'

'Aren't you pleased for them? This means there's a chance that Asia can still have a representative in the last eight.'

'Well, yes, it's good for them, but...'

The train arrives in Shibuya and I find a shop to buy some more beer.

I speak to Kumai, who tells me that Korea have won by scoring a golden goal. They are into the quarter-finals. Japan have been beaten twice today.

A large crowd has gathered outside the station near the statue of Hachiko, a dog that waited at Shibuya Station every day for ten years after his master, whom he used to meet there every day after work, had died from a stroke. The statue there today is a replica, as the original was scrapped during the war to make bombs.

The crowd is young, noisy and wearing Japan shirts and Miyamoto Batman masks.

Some climb into the trees outside the station and lead the others below in chanting.

'Troussier Nippon!'

The cries are valedictory.

I speak to a young couple. He is wearing a Japan shirt and a Batman mask, she a Japan shirt, a bandana and is carrying a white fan with the red of the Hinomaru in the centre. A traditional fan often seen at summer festivals, she has customized hers in white lettering over the Hinomaru, 'Troussier Nippon'.

I ask if they have heard the Korea score.

'Yeah, they won. They did really well.'

'You don't mind?'

'Mind? No, why should we mind? That's good for them.'

'But they have got further then Japan.'

'That means nothing. It's good for them – that's all. Japan did really well. We got through to the second round. This is only our second World Cup. We were great.'

Another fan is carried on his friends' shoulders and placed on the top of the low wall around the trees. On his head he wears a giant football and he has the Hinomaru draped around his back. I ask the couple how they feel to be Japanese tonight.

'*Saiko*! – Brilliant!'

As the young crowd continues to celebrate their new-found love of their flag and their country, decidedly on their own terms, fireworks go off and split the sky into red and silver. Everyone applauds.

The police suddenly appear and drag away the youth who let the fireworks off.

There are howls of protest and a new chant goes up. The same greeting that was used as a farewell to fans leaving the stadium, though this time ironic.

'*Otsukare-sama keisastsu*! Thank you, hard working police!'
Individual shouts display the rebelliousness of the youthful patriots.
'Coppers piss off home!'
'The police rob our taxes!'
The youth that was dragged away re-appears. He sees me taking notes and comes over.

'They took me away for voluntary questioning. I didn't get arrested. They are idiots. I'm a real hooligan. The next time I'll burn all of Shibuya down. My name is Shinji. Remember my *name*!'

Shinji jumps up onto the wall and rejoins the chants. He seems harmless enough.

Shibuya Station is used by more than one million people a day. The police produce signs telling the crowd that they cannot stand here, that it's dangerous to block a thoroughfare. The police are ignored and seem unwilling to break up the crowd.

On the edges of the crowd, a few middle-aged salarymen and female office workers join in, albeit a little warily. They look more a part of the old Japan. The Japan that gave you a job and a desk for life and asked you to play baseball. They seem at odds with Shinji and the others, but join in the chants. This is a wave of nationalism no politician could ride. This is young and spontaneous and looks very healthy. It will probably be over by tomorrow.

Before getting back on the train, the chants are still ringing around Shibuya. I have a last look at the last night of Troussier Nippon, a country that has either just been born, or just gone out of the World Cup on a badly-defended header.

The Road to Yokohama   Second Round   June 15 to June 18

June 15
Germany 1 0 Paraguay
Seogwipo

June 15
Denmark 0 3 England
Niigata

June 16
Sweden 1 2 Senegal
Oita
Senegal win on Golden Goal

June 16
Spain 1 1 Rep. Ireland
Suwon
Spain win 3-2 on penalties

June 17
Mexico 0 2 USA
Jeonju

June 17
Brazil 2 0 Belgium
Kobe

June 18
Japan 0 1 Turkey
Miyagi

June 18
South Korea 2 1 Italy
Daejeon
South Korea win on Golden Goal

we are nippon

19

The Longest Day – Brazil vs. England

Seventy thousand Brazilians live in Aichi and neighbouring Shizuoka Prefecture, the latter home to the Ecopa Stadium where England are about to play Brazil. Trouble flared in the Brazilian community here in 1999. The economy had nose-dived and unemployment was then at a record high of 4.7%. On a housing estate in nearby Nagoya, the large Brazilian population had become unpopular for its late-night barbecues and noisy card games and amid accusations of dangerous driving, right-wing groups started appearing in large vans emblazoned with patriotic slogans and chrysanthemums, an Imperial emblem.

Along with the vans, one evening a group of about 100 right-wing sympathizers gathered on the estate, shouting, 'Brazilians go home!' and waving metal pipes in the air, taunting the Brazilians to come out and fight.

Japan had wanted Brazilian workers to come to do the jobs they didn't want. They thought these workers would be like them, but what they got instead were people from a different, more outgoing culture, whose social welfare and human rights they continue to ignore. A recent survey showed that 25% of the Brazilian population in Japan is unemployed, while 38% said they are unable to send any money home. Of those that work, 43% receive less than two-thirds of the average non-managerial wage and only 62% are covered by health insurance or other social security programs. The foreign workforce is seen as low-paid and disposable.

Internationalisation is not going all that well in the prefectures of Shizuoka and Aichi.

A good percentage of these people have come to Ecopa to cheer on their team. Outside Aino Station, there are more yellow shirts to be seen then white. The area has two local Portuguese newspapers and a special edition of one, *Jornal Tudo Bem*, is being distributed free at the station.

The wind is whirling discarded newspapers and rubbish around outside and girls posing for photographs in front of the floral stadium commemoration have to keep their hair out of their faces with their hands. In Fukuroi World Square, a makeshift marquee next to the station with food and drink stalls, five-a-side competitions, face painting and a display of local dancing, the fans are encouraged to join in.

'Please, why don't you dance together with us?'

Young women doing traditional Japanese dancing, resplendent in kimono, give way to young Brazilian women in crop tops and short shorts doing the samba. I hurry away before anyone thinks of doing a rendition of 'Knees Up Mother Brown'.

Outside, a stall is giving away printed A4-sized England or Brazil flags and a roaring trade is being done in replica England shirts.

Scantily-clad Brazilian women with their national flag painted on their stomachs attract attention from beer-bellied Englishmen with T-shirts that say 'BOLLOCKS'. When I ask if I can take their photograph, the former smile, primp and pose, the latter ask if I'm from the National Criminal Intelligence Service.

I say I'm not.

'Alright then, but don't ask our names.'

I don't.

Could they be from the feared 'second-wave' of fans, who are reported to have got through the net months before the government confiscated passports and ensconced themselves in Thailand, waiting for the second round? The second-wave is said to be the worst of the hooligans and the gossip doing the rounds says that they will wait until England lose before causing any trouble.

Everyone's attention is diverted by a group of Japanese-England fans who arrive. They are wearing St. George wigs and have their faces painted. By this stage of the tournament that is unremarkable, but this group stands out as they are also carrying photographs of the Queen and a copy of the *Sunday Express* from July 31, 1966. The headline, 'How the Lion Roared', reporting the famous English victory from the day before.

Another Japanese fan wears an England wig but has half his face painted in Brazil colours, the other half in England. Two volunteers are giving out paper cranes. One of them holds up a sign.

'This is a small present for you
from our friends
Please keep one!!
For the peace of the world'

Yet another example of extravagant engineering, the approach to Ecopa is via an escalator that turns a corner up a hill, followed by a long approach to another beautiful stadium rising out of the surrounding greenery and hills. People mingle, buffeted by the strong winds.

I get a call from BBC Radio Cambridge and when I comment on the conditions, I have to duck behind a small wall so I can hear the presenter, such is the wind swirling around. Making a panicky radio debut, I tell the early morning listeners in Cambridge that today is a day more suited to the beach. I completely forget to mention the wind.

I meet several Japanese English fans that I've met at previous games. There is a core of us rushing round the country, spending all our money and losing all our sleep. This is my eleventh game and I desperately need a decent kip. I say farewell to an old friend from the Sweden game at Saitama, Aki, who wears red-and-white, candy-striped trousers, a red-and-white knitted hat, a white T-shirt with a red cross that says 'Englandmania' and a huge St. George flag around his neck that flaps in the wind. We promise to meet again in Saitama for the semi- and Yokohama for the final.

Inside the stadium, the support seems even; perhaps there are slightly more England supporters, certainly they are louder. Sweating up in the exposed media tribune, I sit next to a familiar face I used to watch on *Shoot!* on Tyne-Tees television. He and it were rubbish. I feel guilty for ever having let such a thought cross my mind as we chat and the professional commentator turns out to be a thoroughly nice man. He looks down at the pitch, the crowd opposite and around us, and offers the sort of comment we should have heard more often before Sunderland games on *Shoot!*

'This is going to be a nightmare.'

The teams file out and during 'God Save the Queen', Prince Andrew's face appears on the giant screen. He is visibly moved by the crowd's rendition, despite having missed their cue for the fifth game in a row. I feel a strange, sudden surge of pride that makes me uncomfortable. It quickly vanishes as the Brazilian anthem is customarily booed.

The Disneyland announcer runs through the 'Say Yes for Children' piece as everyone ignores her, the theme from *The Great Escape* starts up and the game kicks off.

The commentator squirms.

'Oh, this is going to be a nightmare.'

The opening exchanges on the pitch are tentative, but in the stands, the England Supporters Band is outplaying the samba band, in terms of volume at least. England again lack the rhythmic sense of their opponents. The sweat pours off the spectators.

Brazil have most of the early possession, but the England midfield and defence are solid, restricting them to one chance as Rivaldo shoots straight at Seaman.

After 22 minutes, Heskey punts the ball long for Owen. More hopeful than inspired, the ball careers off Ferreira Lucio's thigh and Owen pounces, lifting the ball over the falling keeper.

The commentator flies out of his seat as all the other journalists around us are glumly silent. The crowd roar, though the celebrations are more muted than at previous games. Brazil continue to dominate possession, but, just when it looks as though England will go in at half-time one-up, Beckham jumps out of a two-man challenge on the line. Edmilson feeds Ronaldinho as he advances from the halfway-line, selling Ashley Cole a dummy then passing to Rivaldo, who tucks it past Seaman. It looks easy.

All around us people are out their seats while the commentator and I exchange expletives.

As the second half kicks off, the commentator is at it again.

'Oh, this is going to be a fucking nightmare.'

He's right, of course.

Scholes needlessly brings down Kleberson from behind and a free-kick is given. Ronaldinho stands over the ball and the England defenders mark the Brazilians who are lined up on the far side of the box, as if they expect a cross. Ronaldinho kicks with the inside of his right foot, as if to curl the ball away from goal and it floats long and high and over Seaman, who is well off his line.

Perhaps it was deliberate, though not even the Brazilian reporters in the press box think that, they look at each other, shrug, pout with their bottom lips and open their palms to the sky, as if to say, 'What was that?'

Perhaps it was just a fluke, perhaps it was a miss-hit. More likely, it was a high cross, carried on the wind.

The Brazilian supporters don't care and they go crazy.

In the stands England are as quiet as they've been all month and on the pitch, it's as if England have remembered just who it is they are playing. They look harried and frightened.

Dyer comes on, hopefully to run at the Brazilian defence. Moments later, England are given a golden opportunity when Ronaldinho is sent off for a challenge on Mills that hardly deserved a red card.

The commentator, who has revealed himself to be rather observant, spots it way before anyone else.

'Ronaldinho, bad tackle, red card – oh, he's given it. Off you go, sunshine!'

Brazil are down to ten men, though it seems that the opposite must have happened. England are completely bereft of ideas, there is no one who can inspire them and they run haplessly around as Brazil are content, and able, to keep the ball.

Dyer's first touch is poor and he gives it away too often. Beckham dives twice in the box, getting neither a penalty nor a yellow card. Sheringham and Vassell come on, but it is too little, too late. The only goals England have scored from open play have come from opposition mistakes or lucky deflections. England don't carve out a single solid chance.

Brazil begin spoiling tactics and Ronaldo is booed for taking ages to walk slowly off when substituted.

The noise from both sides in the stands is about even as the final whistle goes. England's World Cup ends in a rather pathetic way. Presented with a perfect opportunity to claw things back and clear what would have been a route to the final they would have taken without question in May, they simply don't have what it takes, in terms of ability or drive. They deserve to lose.

Seaman is inconsolable after the game, but he isn't really to blame. Without him, they would never have got this far, his saves and a few lucky breaks masking the team's lack of ability.

England do a lap of honour and are warmly applauded. Beckham and Roberto Carlos swap shirts and hug, and Japan finally gets to see Beckham's chest. The cameras record the moment.

I bid the commentator farewell and walking out of the stand, I ask John Barnes, scorer of England's best-ever goal against Brazil, what he thought about Ronaldinho's free-kick.

'He never meant it.'

Outside the ground the fans are counting the cost. Annabelle, Catherine and Richard arrived from London yesterday and are going home tomorrow, spending £4,000 each.

'Value for money.'

Riz, Sako and Abid, English-Asians from Leeds and London have made the same trip, spending £2,000 in the process.

'It was worth it, though, the people here are brilliant.'

They represent a kind of nationalism and pride in their country that would strike many in Japan as odd, a strength of feeling for England that I could never imagine Pak expressing for Japan. If I heard the same sentiments from a beer-bloated, white skinhead, I would feel very uncomfortable. When I hear them express their disappointment, it is oddly comforting.

'The only reason we lost is coz Eriksson isn't English, I'm telling yer.'

'Come on man, you can't say that, that's rubbish, that is.'

'They make fantastic stadiums here. What's wrong with us, why can't we do this at Wembley?'

Three Brazilians come over and apologise.

'We love England, we're sorry. We were just lucky today, that's all.'

The samba band come out of the stadium and everyone rushes over and surrounds them. They seem very at ease with what they are, very natural and they are very good. They seem to have something the English don't, a feeling of well-being that comes from just being Brazilian, a condition that they like to express, to show off. They move down the concourse toward the station, performing complicated movements with confidence and swagger. On the field and off, this is something Brazil do very well.

The England fans going back down the escalator are very quiet, but well-behaved. If anyone is going to cause any trouble, they don't seem to be here. There is no animosity shown to the Brazilian fans, who are sportingly applauded by groups of English fans. They applaud back. The English are very good at losing.

Outside Aino Station the England shirts on sale have gone down in price by a third to ¥2,000 (£11). I try to find one for Kumai, but they are all extra-large. On the train back to Hamamatsu to catch the Shinkansen back to Osaka, I meet Ricky George, who scored the second goal when non-league Hereford knocked Newcastle out of the FA Cup in 1972. It's long overdue, but I shake his hand. He and his companion are wondering whether their wives will have calmed down enough in two years to let them go to Portugal in 2004. If they play like they just have, I suggest, England might not qualify.

20

Minnows – Senegal vs. Turkey

The quarter-final in Osaka that I hoped would be England vs. Japan has turned out to be Senegal vs. Turkey. This would have given very good odds in May.

Senegal, after losing the 2002 Africa Cup of Nations to Cameroon on penalties in February, are in their first-ever World Cup finals. They were disqualified from the 1990 World Cup before it started, as the head of the Senegalese FA forgot to register the team with FIFA. Turkey have qualified for the first time since 1954.

Senegal are managed by another enigmatic Frenchman, Bruno Metsu. He has stood at the dugout with his long hair and suits, looking like he is about to fly off in a helicopter to play a gig with Eric Clapton. Even more of a hero in Senegal than his compatriot Troussier is in Japan, Metsu was awarded the Senegalese Order of Merit. His popularity increased when he turned down a lucrative offer to manage Sedan, one of his former clubs in France. After he converted to Islam in order to marry Rokhaya Ndiaye, his Senagalese wife, a large section of the Senegal press call him Abdul Karim.

In Osaka they face another Islamic nation, Turkey, who, like Senegal, are largely made up of players who play in Europe.

In Nagai Park, some Japanese fans have taken the Turks at their word, and are now supporting Turkey as they 'represent Japan now'. Others are doing the opposite because they beat Japan, and just as many happen to like Senegal. The underdog is as popular in Japan as anywhere.

Both sets of fans have become very popular since arriving from Korea and the face-painting, greeting and taking of photographs continues in the park.

The Lions of Teranga are the neutrals' favourite and chants of 'Senegal! Senegal!' echo around a stadium with some empty seats and a less frenzied atmosphere than greeted the England and Japan games. I can't help wondering how the family of Okamura Osamu, the man who committed suicide before the tournament began, must feel. Senegal have a band and their rhythms are as good as any that have been heard. They don't stop to rest, not even on 21 minutes, when Henri Camara has a goal disallowed for offside. Turkey have most of the possession and deal well with any threats Senegal pose, while missing a couple of good chances themselves.

Senegal show flashes of inspiration in the second half, though Turkey contain them well and can't convert any of their chances. Normal time ends 0-0 and in the fourth minute of extra time, the fresh legs of Ilhan Mansiz, who has only been on the field for 25 minutes, score with a great, swivelling volley. Senegal, who Metsu said would win the World Cup at the first attempt, are out. Turkey go on to a reunion with Brazil.

Outside a group of fans are chanting, 'Senegal, Senegal, Senegal!' Something isn't quite right and the lack of rhythm and monotone of the chant reveal them to be English fans, happily taking a leaf out of the Japanese book and pledging their allegiances wherever it suits them. They shake hands with a Senegalese man in a feathered headdress and at this World Cup of shocks and surprises, nothing seems more normal.

A local elderly couple are watching the crowd.

'Well, look at that, there are all kinds of people here – how interesting.'

The husband goes into a detailed description of how people with different coloured tickets have to go to different station entrances. Long before he finishes, his wife has stolen away and is staring at a man with a Turkish flag painted on his shaven scalp.

'Well I never...'

Before going off to meet Takeuchi and Shintani, I buy them a beer from two *chinpira*-looking men. I ask them how business is.

'Are you making much money?'

'We're making a bloody fortune.'

They are selling beers for ¥300. I attempt a bit of Osaka-style bargaining.

'How much will you charge me for three?'

'A thousand yen!'

I pay ¥900 for three beers and meet Shintani and Takeuchi and we go to a nearby *izakaya*. Inside, shoes have to be removed and put in small, wooden boxes on the wall. Each box has a number. Shintani chooses 14.

'Cruyff.'

Inside the *izakaya*, housed in a non-descript concrete building, but fitted out to look like turn-of-the-century Japan, the Beatles are playing through small loudspeakers above our table.

Earlier that day, Korea have beaten Spain 5-3 on penalties in dubious-looking circumstances. Spain have two goals disallowed and enough flags raised against them for a lengthy semaphore message. Korea, to Takeuchi's and Shintani's disgust, will be playing in the semi-final. Should they win, they'll be playing in Yokohama. There have been calls in the Japanese media, including one by right-wing Tokyo governor Ishihara Shintaro, to support them.

Takeuchi is not impressed.

'If Korea win, they should have the bloody final over there. Only stupid, non-football fans could want them to win. I hate Korea.'

'Yeah, I don't like them much, either.' Shintani joins in, nationalism getting the better of internationalisation as the Beatles sing 'All You Need Is Love'.

Takeuchi explains.

'I hate Korea, not the country or the people, but Japanese football fans can't support the Korean national team. I can't understand people wanting them to win. I just can't understand it. I don't understand about the war or any of that, but as far as football is concerned, Korea have always been our main rivals; they hate losing to us, and we have always thought we have to beat them. When we lose in the World Cup, everyone says we should support them and I'm sorry, but I just can't do that.'

Shintani goes a little bit further.

'I don't like them. Ever since the war, they keep harping on that Japan should apologise, which is a bit rich coming from a military regime. They aren't one now, but that's the way they go on, indoctrinating their own people and blaming things on others. We have to give them aid and I'd just much rather it went to people who needed it, in Africa or Vietnam or wherever.'

'Their football is good, though.' I try to move things on.

'It's too direct, though,' Shintani says, 'just like them…and they never say sorry.'

'Look, we just can't support them, you couldn't support Germany, could you? Not because you hate the people or anything to do with the war, just football.'

'Well, I supported Germany against America.'

'Ah, that's different, everyone wants America to lose.'

As today was the game that we all hoped would see England play Japan on our home turf, I ask them how they feel things have gone. Shintani echoes something Hitoshi had said about poor countries being desperate to win.

'England aren't good because they're too rich.'

'They'll win next time,' Takeuchi adds, 'they're all young. It's true they can't fight to the end, though it's like they don't want to win. I was shocked, they were all rubbish against Brazil. It might have helped if it had rained, but if they looked at the teams left in the tournament, they should have realised it was a golden opportunity to win the whole thing. They should have been running until they threw up.'

Alfred had said the English were just naturally untalented, and could never rise to the big occasion. Takeuchi says the Japanese were similar against Turkey.

'Troussier always said it was a bonus to get to the last 16. I don't understand that. Troussier couldn't be bothered, could he? Maybe the players were trying their best, but it didn't look like it.

'When the team was announced and I heard Nishizawa's name, I thought it was all over. And Alex, he's Brazilian. I can't understand why there is a

159

Brazilian playing for Japan. It was the same before with Ramos and Lopez. I hate them. They're Brazilian, not Japanese, if you look at them, it's obvious. Why are they in the Japanese team? I wouldn't mind if they were Brazilians who were born in Japan, but everyone thought that when Alex joined the team we'd be able to win, just because he's Brazilian.

'I can't understand why he played Nishizawa and not Morishima. I could understand it if he was injured or had a fit like Ronaldo. I wish Nishizawa would bugger off.

'I didn't have a clue what Troussier was doing. Ono wasn't fit and he should have put Nakamura in the squad. As for Troussier, I want him to bugger off as quickly as possible, too.'

I compare Takeuchi to Koizumi, saying they both cried after the Osaka game. Takeuchi snorts.

'Koizumi doesn't really care about football, there's always some politician there. Most of the people watching aren't really football fans, either; they're Japan fans. If Koizumi or a pop star is on the big screen rather than Nakata or Morishima, they're happier. "Look, so-and-so's here watching, too!" It's like five- or six-year olds watching football, they don't know anything.'

I tell them that Koizumi got a huge round of applause at Yokohama during the national anthem. Shintani explains the mixed feelings a lot of people have.

'When I was at school, all the teachers said that "Kimigayo" and the flag belonged to the imperialists before the war, and we shouldn't sing it or raise the flag. I believed them. I used to think singing "Kimigayo" at football games was wrong.

'The young kids who sing it and wear the flag today think it's OK, which it is. I'm Japanese and I want to say I am. There's nothing wrong with it, it has nothing to do with the right wing – that's all over.

'It would be wrong for Ishihara or Koizumi to jump on the bandwagon – everyone would think so. This is about football, not about politics. Of course there is a bit of nationalism in the middle of all the flag-waving at the games, but nobody relates that to fighting for your country. We're not going to join the army. What would I want to do that for?

'There are no right-wing songs like "No Surrender" or "Rule Britannia" that the Japanese fans sing. We just support the football team.'

Agreed that this is the best thing to do, we drink up and leave.

The Road to Yokohama Quarter Finals   June 21 and 22

June 21
England 1 2 Brazil
Shizuoka

June 21
Germany 1 0 USA
Ulsan

June 22
Spain 0 0 South Korea
Gwangju
South Korea win 5-3 on penalties

June 22
Senegal 0 1 Turkey
Osaka
Turkey win on Golden Goal

we are nippon

21

Auntie FIFA

Before arriving at the 'House of Football' as a paying guest, FIFA insists that you wipe your feet. The list of things that can't be taken into the stadiums is long, but includes glass bottles, cans, plastic bottles with lids and sealed cartons. FIFA, in fact, suggest in the *Spectator Guide*, that you arrive carrying nothing – nothing that can be thrown, certainly, and nothing, presumably, that can be eaten or drunk. Don't forget your wallet though, as there will be plenty of things on sale, and do remember to come early, as much as three hours before kick-off if you like, or they won't be able to serve you all the wonderful things they've prepared.

Inside the stadiums beer, a can of the official beer of the World Cup, can be bought for ¥500 (£2.75). The normal price of this beer at a convenience store is ¥240 (£1.32). Half-litre plastic PET bottles of tea, water and other soft drinks are available for ¥250 (£1.37) – normal price: ¥150 (82p). Just in case all this profiteering should create bad press, FIFA and the sponsors attempt to subsidise journalistic opinion by making the same soft drinks available to the media from machines in the press centres for ¥50 (27p).

Didn't you bring your camera? Never mind, our official sponsor will sell you a disposable one for ¥2,000 (£11) and if you've run out of film, we can sell you that, too, for ¥600 (£3.30), 50% more than you could have bought it for yourself if we'd encouraged you to bring a bag to put it in. Film and film processing are available free to members of the press, by the way.

The *Spectator Guide* is a breast-pocket-sized book with a full-colour official sponsor's advertisement on every left-hand page and matronly instructions on the right. It opens at its middle pages with a stern warning about 'ambushing'. Some people, it claims, try to ambush the World Cup for their own profit. They take with them to games articles with unofficial, unauthorized company names and logos on them, trying to get unpaid advertising through a false association with the event. These people, the guide claims, 'don't invest one penny to support the event – they simply rip it off!'

The indignity of the exclamation mark and the choice of phrase, given the pricing policy of food and drinks at the matches is galling. The guide reminds spectators that security will be checking for just such 'ambushing' T-shirts, balloons, banners, scarves and hats etc. and will be removing them at the entrances.

Just in case the message isn't clear enough, the warnings are accompanied by two photographs of the same young England fan hoisting an England flag above his head. In one photo, the flag is unblemished and is accompanied by a large green tick. In the other, the flag says in bold type in three languages, 'Company Name/Logo' and is accompanied by a large red cross. At the top of the page, a small referee holds up a red card.

FIFA controls its image rights so carefully that it tells spectators they cannot take photographs or record any images or sound for the purpose of profit. FIFA, of course, reserves the right to take photographs, record images and sounds of the supporters for the purpose of profit. To allow them to do so without hindrance, spectators are barred from 'disguising one's face, for example, by wearing a mask'. One of the official sponsors of the tournament, handed out free 'Batman' masks, as worn by Japan's Miyamoto to protect his broken nose. The masks, of course, were printed with the sponsor's name and logo. The same sponsor also sold hats that were a replica of the official World Cup football and entirely obscured the wearer's head, though not the company name printed on it.

Profiteering, of course, is not FIFA's goal. That goal is explained on page two of the *Accreditation Handbook* for journalists.

'We believe this event will contribute greatly to our goal: global peace and harmony.'

Sepp Blatter was elected FIFA president in 1998 in Paris after an acrimonious campaign against Lennart Johansson of UEFA. Blatter reportedly offered bribes of up to $100,000 for votes, something he strenuously denies.

In 2001, the collapse of ISL, FIFA's marketing company, with debts of over £750 million, led calls for Blatter's departure. Blatter said he had nothing to hide and an internal investigation into the organisation's finances was made.

Issa Hayatou, the head of the Confederation of African Football, announced he would stand against Blatter for the presidency of FIFA in an election on the eve of the World Cup in 2002. Hayatou, with several high-profile internal backers, promised to clean up FIFA with a policy of transparency. Blatter subsequently cancelled the investigation into FIFA finances, claming that confidentiality had been breached.

A report released by FIFA general secretary Michel Zen-Ruffinen, three weeks before the election, accused Blatter of malpractice and financial irregularities. It said he broke FIFA rules and committed some acts that under Swiss law would be illegal. Blatter countered, saying the Zen-Ruffinen report was flawed and the allegations would come back to haunt those that made them.

At a meeting the day before the election, Blatter was booed by delegates after he refused around 15 people permission to speak against him. Zen-Ruffinen claimed FIFA was not working any more and would have to be rebuilt. Blatter's conduct was variously labelled scandalous, selective and an absolute disgrace.

For his part, Blatter promised to show where FIFA money went. At the next day's election, 195 of the 205 national FAs with a vote were expected to attend. Each association receives at least £250,000 a year, with extra cash from FIFA's Goal project. How many associations would risk exposing their own finances was deemed to be crucial to the vote. Would they prefer a new man asking questions about how they spent their money, or should the status quo remain?

The following day, Blatter was re-elected by 139 votes to 56. Blatter said the vote exonerated him from accusations of corruption. In his valedictory address, Blatter gave thanks for his election after months of being called 'a bad man'.

'You cannot be so bad when this happens. We are all good. Let us now forget what has happened and go forward. FIFA will be one family.'

Blatter then set about splitting FIFA apart. His first target was Zen-Ruffinen. The man he called FIFA's 'Mr. Clean', whom he had once said was like his son, 'mutually agreed' to leave his post on July 4.

The English FA's Adam Crozier said it was bad news for football and that things would get worse. Blatter said it was time to reunite the FIFA family.

If FIFA were a family member, it would be your fussy old auntie.

FIFA owns and runs the largest sporting event in the world and it often feels like the spectators, at least those at the games themselves, are an inconvenience preventing them from working with the people they'd much rather be involved with – the corporate sponsors and the television companies.

FIFA itself acts like a huge corporation, insisting that a copyright and trademark symbol accompany every mention of the World Cup or picture of the trophy. Every effort is made to push the 'brand' and expand into the four corners of the world. Blatter calls China a country with 'huge potential', though it isn't clear whether he means footballing or market potential.

The World Cup attracts more television viewers than any other sporting event, and it is this audience FIFA wants to target. This is well-illustrated by the photograph on page nine of FIFA's official *Magazine* in May 2002. The photograph shows a Malian family of three, sitting on a stone floor in a tiny shack with holes in the roof and a collapsing corrugated iron roof. They are watching football on their television. FIFA sees these people as customers.

This market can be reached far more effectively if countries with weaker national teams, but huge television audiences, qualify. Hence the World Cup was held for the first time in Asia and Blatter said he was 'delighted' that China had qualified.

No doubt the Chinese attending the games in Korea, and watching on television or at home, were equally delighted. China went on to lose all their games, as did Saudi Arabia and Slovenia. Given that FIFA expects, it says, the very best from its referees and players, can the inclusion of sides like Saudi Arabia and China justify the exclusion of the Netherlands or even Wales and Scotland?

FIFA takes a similar attitude to appointing referees and referees' assistants as it does when selecting the host and allocating World Cup places. Spreading the game is the aim. Therefore, at the World Cup in Korea and Japan, the 36 referees and 36 assistants were drawn from the best available on the five continents. That some officiate at the highest level every week, whereas some belong to football associations with only semi-professional leagues, does not seem to matter. Everybody gets their chance. Laudable as this may be, the dubious decisions started from the first whistle.

Reasonable penalty appeals against Japan were turned down. Japan had a goal disallowed against Belgium, Italy had two goals disallowed against Croatia, two more disallowed against Mexico, one against Korea and then Totti was sent off. Spain had two goals disallowed against Korea, Belgium had a goal disallowed against Brazil, the USA had a good penalty appeal turned down against Germany and the talk of a conspiracy grew up.

Some people said that the referees were trying to get the hosts into the final. Others said a Germany vs. Brazil final had been planned from the start, which was why they had such easy groups. After Japan lost to Turkey, there was a rumour that if Korea got through, the final would be moved to Seoul. Blatter made a statement on the FIFA website reiterating the final would be held in Yokohama on June 30 and dismissed any allegations of a conspiracy in favour of Korea.

In his 'World Cup Wish-List' in *Magazine*, May 2002, Michel Zen-Ruffinen, listed 'good refereeing' as his number one wish. Mistakes, he said, were bound to be made, as they were by the players and coaches. All we really want, he said, is consistency.

Although players do make mistakes, they are playing at the very top of their field. All are young, extremely fit athletes, who practice for hours a day. Most are a credit to their profession. Referees and assistants, however, are not universally fit, are not professionals and do not put in the same hours of practice a player does. With an average age of around 40, how can a referee or linesman be expected to keep up with a 23-year old sprinting for the ball?

FIFA acknowledged that major mistakes had been made and said they were determined to improve refereeing standards and selection methods. They again dismissed the use of video replays. Blatter attacked the officials and said the linesmen were a 'disaster'. FIFA got over 400,000 angry emails from Italy after the Korea game and a large number from Spain. Blatter said that from now, officials should be appointed on ability not nationality.

It can only be hoped the same attitude prevails in deciding the qualifying round for Germany 2006.

we are nippon

22

Semi-Final in The Pub – Germany vs. Korea

The Pub is an unimaginatively named pub in Osaka, close to Namba Station. The Pub used to be a restaurant, but when the owner went bankrupt, spotting an opportunity, the landlord of Murphy's Irish bar in Shinsaibashi stepped in. With something of a reputation as a tight-fisted moneygrabber, whether deserved or not, his idea was to show all the World Cup games on big screens, advertise in the local English-language press and on World Cup-related websites, attracting foreigners living in, and visiting Japan for the World Cup. Here they could drink familiar beers and eat familiar food, while watching the games with the comforting, familiar voices of John Motson and Barry Davies doing the commentary, relayed via SKY PerfecTV, a Murdoch-controlled satellite station that was broadcasting every match free of charge. The catch being, of course, that it is necessary to buy a decoder and start a contract with SKY PerfecTV.

None of this would need to worry the customers at The Pub, though, which would be laying it all on. All the customers would have to worry about would be the price of their bar bill. Pints of Guinness, Kilkenny's and lager are sold at ¥850, around £4.60 each. A plate of fish and chips costs ¥700, around £3.80. When a plate arrives, the fish turns out to be two frozen fillets, six of which can be bought in the supermarket for ¥300, accompanied by eight chips. At FIFA World Cup 2002 Korea/Japan™, everyone is after their pound of flesh.

The Pub, of course, is packed every night as the sizeable contingent of sizeable Englishmen continue their re-fuelling.

This is also where Takeuchi said he would prefer to watch the semi-final between South Korea and Germany. I would much rather go somewhere quiet, away from the crowds of Englishmen, though I can hardly protest. Besides, this is supposed to be an international event.

I arrive just before kick-off. Pak, Shintani and Takeuchi are already there, expensive glasses in hands. Takeuchi and a woman with him are wearing Bayern Munich shirts. She must be one of the two girlfriends he mentioned in the *izakaya* the other night. They seem an unlikely match, him all chubby, gruff-straight-forwardness and opinions and her small, quiet and demure. A thought about them together with football kits on briefly plays itself into my mind, but then I'm saved from myself by Alfred's hurried arrival. For a few moments, he doesn't see us and looks menacing as he squints around the bar, puzzled, alternately raising his eyebrows then narrowing his eyes. He spots us and his face explodes into a wide grin, a grin that becomes even wider when he realises what Takeuchi and his companion are wearing. He makes a beeline for her.

'Bayern Munich. Splendid. I am from Munich and Bayern Munich are my team. You have chosen well.'

I tell them that Alfred used to be a goalkeeper in a Bayern youth team. Everyone is impressed and lets it be known with the expulsion of a single, hummed syllable that rises in pitch, sounding like a question.

'E-e-e-e-e-e-h?'

'I have to say I was pretty good; we always won the championship. We had a very good forward. I heard he's playing somewhere in the Bundesliga. I heard that one made it. I had a good time. Playing football was a lot of fun. When you stop a ball and everyone says "Well done!" it's great.'

Everyone, except Pak, is supporting Germany. This is not the kind of link that were supposed to be forged by co-hosting. Takeuchi explains how everyone feels.

'It'll be a Germany win, Korea have just been lucky because of the refs.'

I mention that Japan's star midfielder, Inamoto, has been on television that evening and said that he hoped that the Japanese supporters would now get behind Korea.

'He's a nice lad, though,' says Takeuchi, 'I'm not. I definitely won't support Korea.'

'I'm not a nice lad, either,' adds Shintani, 'I just want to see a good game.'

Takeuchi sits down some feet away and Shintani stands further back. I move nearer the television; Pak is seated directly in front of me and Alfred away to the right. The bar is loud and I ask Pak what he thinks of Takeuchi in his Bayern kit.

'Well, yes, it looks like he hates us.'

'But you've supported Japan, haven't you?'

'Well, yes, but that's just me. Takeuchi is Takeuchi.'

I raise my voice and turn toward Takeuchi.

'If Korea win and they come to Japan for the final, would you support them?'

Takeuchi looks shocked.

'You're joking, aren't you? Absolutely no way! If that happens, they should have the bloody final in Korea!'

Takeuchi's spirit of internationalism doesn't seem to stretch to Korea.

The game kicks off and both Pak and Alfred are visibly nervous. An early decision goes to Korea.

'Is he Korean?' Alfred wants to know, pointing at the referee, 'I thought he was Swiss. The Swiss should like us because we gave them lots of money during the war.'

From another part of The Pub, the area directly in front of the bar come shouts of '*Dae Han Min Guk*! – The Republic of Korea!' They don't sound like Korean or Japanese people, though as we have commandeered an area in front of the biggest screen, I can't see. I suspect they are English.

At least Pak isn't alone. I feel a little sorry for him, it must be disheartening, never mind confusing, given that your country of birth, which gives you its language and culture, rejects you as a citizen, forcing a different nationality on you, which is then encouraged by your schooling. Your friends and colleagues, meanwhile, who wouldn't know from looking at you or hearing you speak that you were Korean unless you told them, all make their feelings of enmity toward your country of nationality very, very obvious.

I am supporting Korea – partly in sympathy for Pak, partly as they have done well to get this far, partly because they are also the underdog, but mainly because the opposition just happens to be the Germans.

On eight minutes, Lee Chun-Soo forces Oliver Kahn into making a great save.

'*Dae Han Min Guk*!'

'He is a great keeper.' Alfred shouts, nodding to himself.

The Germans continue to put the Koreans under pressure, peppering the Korean box with crosses, searching for their forwards and trying to make the most of their height advantage.

Pak is completely silent, writhing and twisting in his chair, covering his face with a World Cup towel he has draped round his neck whenever things get too much to look at.

A Korean free-kick goes wide to further Pak's misery.

'Don't put it there!'

A Korean player goes down and seems to be staying down too long for Takeuchi's discerning eye.

'Get up, you soft git!'

A goalmouth scramble before half-time sees Pak under his towel for several anguished seconds before the half-time whistle goes. Alfred nips out to the *pachinko* parlour next door to use the toilets, while Takeuchi sums up his feelings on the first half.

'This is boring. It's nothing like a semi-final.'

While Pak is comparing the age, functions and weight of his mobile phone with a stranger seated nearby, I ask Alfred on his return from the toilet how he feels things are going.

'We shall see. So far there have been 60,000 people and the referee playing for the Koreans. They do not deserve to be in the semi-finals – the quarter-finals, yes, but not the semis. I feel sorry for the Spanish,' he says,

171

referring to their disallowed goals. Everyone agreed the decision had been a terrible one and the Spanish were unfortunate.

'How about the Americans?' I ask, 'Wasn't that a handball on the line that kept them out of the game?'

'The rules say if you don't move your hand, it isn't a handball, and he didn't move his hand,' Alfred explains with a ruthless, efficient interpretation of the rules. The camera zooms in on a spectator holding the German flag. Alfred had sung the national anthem, but I suspect he was playing to the crowd.

'The national anthem is a nice song. I like the music. When I see the German flag in a football stadium I'm proud, because Germany play well. I only wave the German flag during the World Cup. I prefer the Bavarian flag. I feel more Bavarian than German. I don't like the Prussians. All that goose-stepping and Nazism, that was the Prussians. I'm German, I have a German passport, but I don't care where anyone is from. Germans? Aryans? There are no Aryans. It's a big mix.'

Alfred's take on German nationalism is comforting, but then he spoils it by mentioning the war.

'Klose's father played for Poland. Half the German population came from France, Spain and Sweden. The Huguenots came from France. Neuville must be a Huguenot. Hans Joachim Marseille, the German fighter ace from WWII, his ancestors were French.'

Everyone applauds the re-start and Alfred eyes me.

'Hey, Simon, the referee looks like Steve McQueen.'

He raises his eyebrows, grins, twitches and nods three times at me as if I should understand some oblique reference he is making – again he looks momentarily menacing. Perhaps he's referring to *The Great Escape*. Perhaps he's hinting that the Germans held the Americans prisoner and try as they might, they couldn't escape. I haven't got a clue, and the referee looks nothing like Steve McQueen.

Guus Hiddink, whose positive tactics have been a definite high spot, has brought on Ahn Jung-Hwan for Hwang Sun-Hong and Lee Min-Sung for Choi Jin-Chul. Korea look set to attack.

They push forward, but the German back line stands resolute, refusing to be broken down.

On 70 minutes, Lee Chun-Soo dances past several German defenders only to be brought down cynically by Michael Ballack. There are boos from near the bar and cheers from near me. Pak stares at the television screen, agog.

Alfred preempts German manager Rudi Voeller who will later concur in a television interview. 'It was a professional foul, he had to do it or they would have scored. He placed himself at the service of the team and the whole of Germany.'

Whether this exact thought had crossed Ballack's mind, only he will ever know. Perhaps it was an intentional, goal-saving foul, or perhaps it was just an instant reaction. Either way, Ballack has sacrificed himself for the good of the team. He receives a yellow card, his second of the tournament and should Germany progress, he will miss the final. Voeller, meanwhile, confirmed what everyone has long suspected, that the Germans are cynical, cold-hearted and ruthless.

Five minutes later, Alfred again has to go to the neighbouring *pachinko* parlour to relieve himself. Quite naturally, when he is away, Germany score.

Judging from Voeller's later comments about the necessity of the foul, it is difficult to say that Ballack went from villain to hero in five minutes, to some he was hero and hero again. To the Koreans, a villain then a devil. Neuville moves cleverly down the right and pulls back for Ballack, whose first effort is saved by the keeper. The rebound runs kindly for the Germans and Ballack slots home with his second stab.

Germany 1, Korea 0.

Takeuchi, his girlfriend and Shintani all cheer while Pak groans and disappears under his towel.

By now, all the surrounding tables have realised they have a real live German amongst them. When Alfred returned from the pachinko parlour, he is eyed by half The Pub back to his seat, where he is told that Germany have scored.

Alfred squints again, eyeing the score in the screen's top-right corner.

'Ha, ha, ha! Deutschland!'

Pak continues his silent writhing.

Bode takes a free-kick for Germany and almost doubles their lead. Korean keeper Lee Woon-Jae, dives to his left and punches the shot away.

'Deutschland!' yells Alfred.

'Deutschland!' yells Takeuchi.

'Deutschland!' yells everyone.

Pak writhes.

Late in the game, Park Ji-Sung gets free inside the box, only to shoot wide, wasting a definite chance.

Pak again hides under the towel.

The Koreans look tired. They look as if they have finally run out of ideas. As the final whistle blows, Pak lets out an anguished sigh.

'Aghhh! It's all over.'

Alfred beams with delight.

'I am glad that we won. Their keeper said that he would defend his goal easily. They were too confident. Spain, Italy and Portugal all lost. They have 60,000 supporters behind them, but Germans are mentally very strong at times like that. It was a wonderful sight to see Korea play attacking football when they went behind, but send them to Europe and they'll lose.

'I hope the Turks beat Brazil – the back-stabbers. They dive all over the place and hold their faces. I don't know how you didn't beat them. Maybe it's because England never fought a war against Brazil – it should have been Argentina. You don't win anything because you aren't good at football. You need someone with a brain who can pass. Owen's goal was a present. The goal for 1-1 was a nice pass, but 2-1 was just bad luck. I felt sorry for Seaman, but he was too far out. You have a lot of good players, but why didn't they score against only ten Brazilians? I won't say, "See you in Germany," because you won't qualify.'

Pak congratulates Alfred and wishes Germany well in the final.

'I wanted to win of course, but I didn't think we would. We had no energy left. I wanted Korea to win, not because I wanted them to do better than Japan, I don't feel any complex toward Japan. We'll both be hopeless at the next World Cup, so it was good to go as far as we could this time. I didn't think for a moment, "Ha, ha! We got further than you!" Not even a little bit, honestly!

'Korea got to the last four and Japan to the last 16. Japanese people say we only got through because of the ref's mistakes. It just shows the ridiculousness of Japan-Korea relations. The whole thing's stupid. I hated the campaign in Japan for the Japanese to support Korea, why bother? Just leave people alone to support who they want. I doubt there were people in Korea supporting Japan.'

Takeuchi later sends Pak an email to say that it would have been nice for Korea to win. In defeat, international relations are much easier.

Pak thinks the attitude of the Italians and Spanish shows a superior European attitude toward Asia, leaving them blaming the referees.

'Maybe for European teams, losing to an Asian team was just too much to take and they wanted an excuse. The games are over and there's nothing you can do now. The Spain goal-line mistake and when Totti was sent off, they were pretty bad, but it was funny when the Italians thought the ref was the enemy.'

I leave, but call in to see Hitoshi on the way home. He has some thoughts on the Korean crowd.

'They're just joining in for the sake of it. The people who go to the Korean games don't care about football. They just go there to enjoy the World Cup, the event. They just want their country to win, they hate other countries. They are devastated when they lose.

'They were really strong, though, I wonder if they were taking drugs. They've always taken drugs.

'It was a mistake to have the tournament in Asia. In the humidity there's nothing you can do, you can't run, you're knackered after ten minutes and your body can't get rid of the sweat. They should play it in South America or Europe where it belongs.

'When Italy lost to Korea, they lost to Asia and couldn't get over it, so they have to blame the referee. Spain, too, but that happens at home, there was a home advantage, of course there was. The referees were terrible mind, that was another huge mistake, giving those referees a job.'

A customer comes in and Hitoshi goes back to slicing fish. I go home to pack. Tomorrow I'm going back to Kanto.

we are nippon

23

Saitama Samba – Brazil vs. Turkey

Another day following the World Cup, another Shinkansen to Tokyo and another five hours on three trains. At Omiya Station, the
volunteers are the best organised I've come across yet. The one I
ask at the station for the media bus has no hesitation in directing me in
Japanese to the volunteer whose job it is to take care of the privileged
press. The shuttle buses leave from around the corner from the station and
I'm guided by a volunteer. We walk up a set of steps and another level of
streets presents itself. Most areas around stations in Japan are busy, and
are therefore prime real estate. The city planners see no point in stopping
at building up either side of the roads. They build down underneath, creating shopping malls that go on for miles in every direction. Above ground
they construct walkways, with more access to more shops. We walk a cir-
cuitous route around a few of these before descending some steps to the
bus stops.

There is a crush of the world's media waiting and colourful language of
all international hues drifts up into the walkways. The buses are delayed.
We are given tickets with a number and asked to wait in line. When the
bus arrives, it is obvious that there are more people holding numbers than
there are seats available. The bus fills up and the volunteer staff announce
the rest of us will have to wait for the next bus that will be here in 45
minutes.

A large Brazilian man shouts that his piece of paper has no meaning
and throws it onto the ground. As he pushes his way onto the bus, a volunteer rushes to pick up his discarded slip of paper. Everyone follows him
onto the bus until there is no one left waiting and the bus is dangerously
full.

The driver protests, but no one moves. We pull off, lacking only a goat,
some chickens and a few baskets of eggs to complete the feeling of travelling into town to go to market.

I go through the airport-style security and change my pitch ticket for
one in the stand. I don't even bother to check when the photographers'
briefing was – missing it is now as much a part of my routine as my pre-
match 'special coffee' and half-time official beer.

Inside, Saitama Stadium is decked out in yellow. Brazil, having completely stolen England's thunder, are the home team now. A Turkish minor-

ity can be heard in the breaks when the samba stutters, but most neutrals are supporting Brazil. There are again some empty seats in a prime viewing section in the top tier of the stand opposite the team benches.

Every time Brazil touch the ball, they are urged on by huge roars, but Turkey play well and after 20 minutes have the first clear chance from a free-kick when Marcos pushes an Alpay header round the post.

Brazil hit straight back and almost score twice in a minute. A Cafu shot hits Recber Rustu in the Turkey goal and then bounces over the bar. Roberto Carlos then shoots wide as the semi-final turns into a great game. Rivaldo miscues and Ronaldo tries to poke home from the edge of the six-yard box, but Rustu smothers the ball to see five chances in five minutes.

Turkey continue to press, but Rivaldo has two chances for Brazil inside a minute and the samba band play up a storm.

Just before half-time, Rustu makes a tremendous save at the feet of Rivaldo, who kicks him in the head for his troubles. While the game is stopped, Ronaldo pushes a Turkish player and several more from both sides join in, pushing and shoving each other like kids in the playground.

Four minutes into the second half, Ronaldo turns Fatih Akyel and goes past Bulent Korkmaz to stab the ball in with his toe. Rustu is finally beaten. Ronaldo is now the leading scorer with six goals.

After Brazil score, the Turks seem to lose heart and run out of ideas. Brazil press for 20 minutes and should go two up as Kleberson, and then Edilson, miss, as Turkey leave holes in defence in their efforts to push up.

It has turned cold and as the game enters the last 20 minutes, half of me wants Turkey to score and half wants to get away early. Either way, with Turkey playing the way they are now, a goal is not likely. Brazil have more chances and Turkey go close with just over ten minutes to go. Brazil do not look like surrendering their lead.

In the last minute, Denilson wins a free-kick with a dive. There is some truth in what Alfred says. The Brazilians' football has been wonderful at times, but they dive, roll around and waste time at substitutions when they are in front. It is unbecoming of players of such skill. Ilhan misses Turkey's last chance – a free header from 10 yards out – and the whistle goes for full-time. Brazil are in their third consecutive final.

The crowd loves them and when the final whistle goes, the yellow hordes go crazy. Drums and whistles pound and shrill the stadium atmosphere. Outside the fans gather in the space between the stadium gates and the queues for the buses, waiting for the samba band. The Brazilians coming out of the gate present themselves in the full array of colours that makes up their country.

A blonde woman with milky white skin wraps herself in the Brazil flag and does an impromptu solo samba for the cameras. She is joined by men who want to kiss her and she grants them all their wish.

A Japanese-Brazilian couple speak Portuguese and Japanese as they pose for photos. A black Brazilian man takes a photo of a southern European-looking Brazilian woman. She has long dark hair and has the Brazil flag painted on her heavily pregnant stomach which pokes out from under her cropped top. A camera crew appears and she dances a furious samba.

The samba band pour out of the gate. The feathered headdresses, the drums, whistles and percussion lead a victory parade to the station.

To the right, a dejected troupe of Turks march a rolled flag back to their bus. They are warmly applauded. They wave back and then disappear. They will go back to Seoul for the third-place play-off.

Brazil, meanwhile, have a date on Sunday with Germany at the Yokohama International Stadium.

The Road to Yokohama   Semi-Finals   June 25 and 26

June 26
Brazil 1 0 Turkey
Saitama

June 25
Germany 1 0 South Korea
Seoul

we are nippon

24

The World Cup Final – Brazil vs. Germany

Before I set off for the final, Alfred had asked me to support Germany for him and summed up Germany's World Cup.

'German football is good, it's not very exciting, but if you win, you win. Nobody expected us to get to the final. We got to the final because of Kahn; he's the best keeper and best player in the tournament.

'Saudi was an easy game, but we were wonderful, even so. Ireland were good. When Keane scored, I thought, "Oh my god, now we have to play Cameroon and win." At one-nil I wasn't convinced, at two-nil – yes.

'Paraguay – the bald-headed Paraguay keeper – 1-0 in the last four minutes. America were good – very fast and without Kahn, we would have lost. Ballack scored and Kahn made some great saves – I was on edge. Torsten Frings didn't move his arm for the handball and it wasn't a penalty. We were lucky. Kahn would've saved the day in a penalty shoot-out, though.

'Then we beat Korea. Spain, Italy and Portugal had all lost. Losing against them would've been very bad. They're not such a good team. Anyway, Germany won.

'We've played in two less competitions than Brazil, but we have been in as many finals. If we win this time, it will be four trophies each.'

Outside Yokohama International Stadium, a flame burns. The fans are drawn toward it, their faces painted, their flags draped around their shoulders, their team colours on.

The media shuttle bus once more goes into the bowels of the stadium, but this time is stopped by a team of security guards who check the underside with mirrors.

The media centre is as packed as the stands. Photographers and journalists wait for any unused tickets for the media tribunes. Nobody wants to miss out. Outside, tickets are changing hands for more than ¥500,000, over £2,700.

The opening ceremony features a giant Mount Fuji and volunteers jumping up and down with the flags of the world, whipping up the crowd. All around the stadium, people have brought their own flags: Brazil, Germany, Japan, England, Cuba, Scotland, Wales, Malaysia, the 'rising sun', the Union Jack, the Stars and Stripes, the British Ensign, Wales, Canada, Venezuela, Israel and New Zealand all hang, covering the concrete. This is the international stadium, this is internationalisation.

A group of children from Yokohama and the Tokyo International School line up behind each goal and the crowd is asked, again, to join FIFA and UNICEF in saying yes for children. The children lead the crowd, as the announcer from Disneyland cranks up the phony enthusiasm. She asks the crowd to make ten pledges for children.

'Say Yes For Children!'
'Leave No Child Out – say yes!'
'Put Children First – say yes!'
'Care for Every Child – say yes!'
'Fight HIV and AIDS – say yes!'
'Stop Harming and Exploiting Children – say yes!'
'Listen to Children – say yes!'
'Educate Every Child – say yes!'
'Protect Children from War – say yes!'
'Protect the Earth for Children – say yes!'
'Fight Poverty: Invest in Children – say yes!'

'Thank you for joining us in saying yes for children. Now, let's give a big round of applause for the children.'

The crowd, numb to the announcer after the first two or three pledges, is slow to join in the applause, though most do when they realise it means the woman has shut up.

Next up, after a *Love United - Fight Against Aids* promotional video, is one featuring the Spheriks, the official World Cup mascots. Kaz, Ato and Nik fight the good football fight against evil that tries to corrupt them. Kaz, Ato and Nik are space-age characters; cute, animated things that look suspiciously like they are targeted at children. Toy dolls of the characters can be bought at the souvenir stands and via the official online store where FIFA offers purchasers the opportunity to 'identify with the event and to get a personalised experience.' Say 'Yes!'

The goalkeepers come out to warm up and get a thunderous reception. I realise that I am at the World Cup final.

The screen tells us who is sponsoring what and that tobacco kills, so we shouldn't be duped. We are then treated to a full roll-call of the official sponsors and again told that every child has the right to play and the 2002 World Cup is dedicated to children. It is a long, long time since I have listened to this much sermonisng on a Sunday.

The players come out to warm up and the Germans look big and powerful in their brilliant white strips. They make long strides over the pitch, whipping passes to each other. The Brazilians look smaller, but are working the ball around in small, neat triangles and practising their juggling skills.

After the players go back inside, their names are called and their faces shown on the screens. The Ro-Ri-Ro trio gets the loudest cheers, except from the Germans, who boo Rivaldo. There are more Brazil supporters, though the Germans can easily be heard.

After a thunderous drum roll, Vangelis' 'Anthem' starts up, signalling the teams to come out again. The reception they get is deafening. It is difficult to concentrate. The teams line up and both anthems are well sung. As England aren't here, there is no booing.

The white of Germany lines up against the yellow of Brazil. The whistle blows and the 2002 World Cup final kicks off.

Ronaldinho flies straight down the wing and wins a corner, which goes out for a goal-kick.

Ronaldo shows some neat skills and Germany get in a cross and within eight minutes, Roque Junior for Brazil and Klose for Germany are in Collina's book.

The game has been billed as Kahn versus Ronaldo, but it is Germany who press forward more, their passing crisp and accurate. Brazil are on the back foot, though look dangerous when they break. Carlos juggles the ball out of the corner and the samba band is in full swing.

Ronaldinho slips the ball behind the German defence and Ronaldo is clear. He puts the ball past Kahn, but it goes wide of the post.

The game goes a little flat, the battle being done in midfield. Somewhere amongst the German fans, an inappropriate chant goes up.

'Engerland, Engerland, Engerland!'

Some people just won't go home.

Germany keep possession at the back. The crowd boo when they pass back to Kahn. This is German football as Alfred described it. It isn't pretty, but who cares, if you win? I get the feeling that Brazil don't approve.

Germany are running the game and win another corner. Jeremies tries a long shot and then Kleberson hits the bar for Brazil. This seems to wake them up and Lucio turns in the box and then Ronaldo turns and shoots, only for Kahn to save as he races from his line.

I am at the World Cup final, and it's great.

At the beginning of the second half, Jeremies heads in from the six-yard line, but Edmilson keeps the ball out. Neuville hits a free-kick from 35 yards, which curls in the air, looking like a goal, but Marcos pushes it onto the post.

Ronaldo wins a corner at the other end and Kahn makes a tremendous point-blank save from Rivaldo's resulting header.

Germany have plenty of possession and Frings and then Hamann both shoot over. This is the best World Cup final there has been for years.

The samba band wake up and urge Brazil on.

Brazil win a free-kick and then Carlos gets free, but both come to nothing.

Neuville can't connect with a shot. Jeremies goes off for a minute and when he comes back on, Ronaldo dispossesses Hamann. Rivaldo shoots from 25 yards. Kahn looks like he'll collect, but then fumbles. The ball bounces off his chest and Ronaldo pounces to slot it away.

One-nil to Brazil.

The crowd go mad, though the stadium is so big and the opposite stands so far away, the cheering is lost somewhere in mid-air. The stands with samba bands – there are three – are alive to the sound of drumming.

Marcos pushes a German corner away, Klose goes off and Germany put in cross after cross, though they can't break down what two weeks ago was called a dodgy defence.

Suddenly, Kleberson moves inside and crosses low. Rivaldo dummies, stepping over the ball, which runs onto Ronaldo. Another man who completes a turnaround from four years ago, Ronaldo calmly picks his spot and slots the ball past Kahn and into the corner. That, surely, is that.

The intensity of the samba increases, now with the swagger of a dance of victory.

Bierhoff shoots, but Marcos again saves well. Germany are running out of time. Marcos fluffs a high ball, but Metzelder misses from five yards.

Ronaldinho trudges off slowly when substituted, but is hurried along by Collina.

The shouts echo around the stadium.

'Brazil! Brazil!'

Ronaldo goes off to a crescendo of applause and cheering. A huge grin on his face and the worst haircut in football on his head.

Brazil, to their credit, look for number three.

Ziege has a shot, but it is too late.

The final whistle blows.

There are flashes all around the ground and flags wave furiously. Perhaps because of the size of the ground and the distance of the crowd from the pitch, the cheering is quieter than I had expected; there is no huge roar or explosion, tens of thousands of vocal chords straining together. Perhaps it's because there are so many women and children in the crowd. Perhaps it's because the majority of the crowd are Japanese, and it doesn't have any real meaning for them.

Ronaldo is announced as man of the match as another advert plays noisily on the giant screens at either end, dominating the proceedings as the sponsors share the winners' glory.

As the Brazilian team gathers to celebrate, the Germans are slumped on the ground in the typical pose of the vanquished. Kahn, solid as a rock until today, is alone, as the keeper always is, slumped against the posts he couldn't defend.

The Brazilians begin their lap of honour, though they can hardly be seen for the mass of light blue- and red-bibbed photographers that surround them like a pack of sharks hounding their prey. From the tunnel, three giant paper cranes are carried to the centre of the pitch, where a podium is built in under three minutes. Kahn jumps over the advertising hoardings and goes over to the German fans, who applaud him generously.

The Brazilian lap of honour continues, hampered by the photographers, one cameraman going as far as pushing his intended target backwards so he can get a better shot. Others direct the players to wave their hands over their heads. The celebration has to look right in the papers tomorrow.

The footballing politicians in place, the award ceremony begins.

The Germans walk slowly around the ground, receiving generous applause from both sets of fans and the neutrals. Ronaldo, isolated from his team, is pursued by photographers, who are pushing him to stop him, insisting he raise his Brazilian flag above his head, giving them their shot. He eventually gets free and joins the rest of his team who are gathered in a circle, kneeling to the right of the podium, linking hands and praying.

The referees are presented with their medals by women in kimono.

Germany, the 'silver medallists', the PA announces, take the podium to receive their medals and commiserations. The Brazilians rise from their prayers to huge cheers and some officials from the Brazilians' party carry a banner around the ground, thanking the supporters.

Away to the left, a fan jumps from the seating, over the fence and the trench, onto the covered running track and makes a break for the pitch. He is tackled by several security guards and wrestled to the ground, where he is smothered, restrained and taken away.

The Brazilians take to the podium, most of them wearing the national flag. Each of them receives hugs and kisses from Pele and their medals. Cafu clambers up onto the plinth on the podium.

Pele gives him the trophy.

Fireworks explode into the air. Silver paper is thrown everywhere and above the crowd, the skies erupt with thousands upon thousands of paper cranes, raining down like a monsoon. They are blown out of pipes over the roof of the stand and fall from huge canvas bags up in the gods, drifting slowly, gracefully down, covering everywhere they touch in a multi-coloured paper carpet. Each piece is printed with 2002 FIFA World Cup ©1999 FIFA™. People all around pick up the cranes to take away as souvenirs. FIFA cannot, will not, miss this opportunity to spread its brand name ever further.

As the cranes fall, the extended version of Vangelis' 'Anthem' blasts from the speakers. Ending in choral passages, the religious overtones are hard to miss. The House of Football is a very broad house.

Brazil begin another lap of honour, this time with the trophy. The Germans again take up the positions of the defeated, slumped on the pitch, unable to join in the celebrations, but unwilling to leave the theatre.

As Juninho takes the trophy over to the crowd, ten minutes after they first started floating down, the cranes are still coming, lying inches-deep on the glass roof of the VIP stand. People begin to shuffle away, trampling the cranes underfoot like autumn leaves.

The screens above them read, 'Sayonara, Auf Wiedersehen, Deutschland 2006.'

Outside the stadium, the volunteer staff line the exits and paths, shouting their now normal greetings as they smile for the last time.

'Thank you!'

They give high-fives and wave a hand either side of their head, adding in high-pitched voices as the fans of the world go home.

'Bye-bye!'

'Bye-bye!'

The rain is coming down heavily outside, though Brazilian spirits aren't damped. Some German face paint is seen running down a cheek. Is it the rain or a tear?

On the footbridge that leads over from the stadium to the adjoining street, people gather and dance, jump and sing. The jumping is so fierce that the bridge is shaking, fooling me for a moment into thinking that there is an earthquake.

Did Brazil just shake the world?

Epilogue

Brazil won their fifth World Cup. They were written off before the tournament started, but it was no surprise when they won. There were many, many other surprises, though, and theirs was not the only victory.

Japan and Korea will certainly be looked on in a different, more positive light by the rest of the world that watched them gather in the streets and jump from their bridges. Korea and Turkey were the surprise teams. They went further than anybody could have expected and made new names for themselves.

England made a new name for themselves, too, or rather lived up to their old one as gentlemen. Not one England fan was arrested for public disorder and a survey by an Osaka company also found that 56% of women were said to feel more friendly towards England as a result of the World Cup.

There was trouble, but really very little. A total of 93 World Cup-related arrests were made – 60 of these were Japanese people, and only 13 were British.

J.League attendances into July are vastly up. The question is how long will they last. Membership is also up at the Osaka Supporters Club – female membership in particular. Takeuchi says it will be nice if a few of them stay on.

At Mohejitei, Hitoshi won another small fortune at horse racing and has refitted the counter in marble.

Alfred is establishing a new website giving free legal advice to foreigners.

Pak is looking forward to Germany 2006. He is studying English, so that, trilingual, he can cover it as a reporter. Shintani wants to work in England.

The Osaka survey also found that the World Cup helped people communicate with those around them in society and in their family.

Takeuchi may be cynical enough to only say the only effect on Japan-Korea relations is that there are more Korean pickles in the supermarket, but Japan and Korea have proved they can work together. Takeuchi doesn't seem the sort of man to pay much attention to shopping anyway. Japan is experiencing a 'Korean boom'. Interest in the language and culture have soared.

Many agreed that the tournament was too long. There were too many stadiums and the players were all too tired after too long a domestic season.

Everyone I spoke to who visited the World Cup in Japan, a few cynical journalists excepted, spoke in superlatives. 'I love this country. What a wonderful place. What nice people. Fantastic, tremendous, the best days of my life.'

None of them are likely to be around again long enough for the negative side of things to bother them. None of them, unlike Pak, will really ever have to question what their nationality is, what it means and whether it's a good or bad thing.

There is a move in some political circles to allow foreign permanent residents to vote in local elections. Pak may one day even get full voting rights.

Japan and Korea may both qualify for Germany 2006. England may start playing a new version of total football and beat Germany 3-0 in the final.

FIFA, one day, may achieve, its true goal – world peace.

Peace through war.

Notes

Chapter 10
1 - In 1969, El Salvador invaded Honduras after Honduran landowners deported several thousand Salvadorans. Five-thousand people ultimately died in what became known as the Football War because it broke out during a soccer game between the two countries. They were playing a three-leg World Cup qualifier. Fighting broke out during the first game in Tegucigalpa, but the situation got considerably worse during the second match in San Salvador. Honduran fans were beaten up, the Honduran flag and national anthem were insulted and the emotions of both nations became considerably heated.

Glossary of Terms

Banzai! – hooray! (lit. 10,000 years)
bento – a packed or boxed lunch either prepared at home or bought from a shop

chijimi – Korean savoury pancake
chinpira – low-ranking gangsters

Dae Han Min Guk – The Republic of Korea (Korean)
daijobu – no problem

furigan – Japanese rendering of hooligan(s)

Gambatte! – Do your best! Get stuck in! Encouragement said to anyone for just about any reason
gaikokujin torokusho – alien registration card
geppu – burp

Heian Period (AD 794-1185) – an aristocratic age of peace when the arts flourished
Hinomaru – the Japanese flag; literally, the round of the sun

ii – good
izakaya – the closest thing the Japanese have to a pub; a place where drinks and food are served

kakkoii – cool
Kampai! – Cheers! (lit. 'dry glass')
Kanto – the eastern area of Honshu (Japan's largest island) includes Tokyo
kiken – dangerous
kimchi – spicy Korean pickled vegetables
'*Kimigayo*' – the Japanese national anthem
kitanai – dirty
kitsui – difficult, tough
kokusai kekkon – international marriage
konnichiwa – good day, hello
-kun – junior, a term of familiarity

makase – let someone else do something
makizushi – sushi rolled in dried seaweed
mama-san – female boss of a bar
manbiki – shoplifting
Mansei! – the Korean equivalent of *Banzai!*
mecha – very
muko – over there, a place or country far away

naijin – mainlander, old, derogatory term used by people from Hokkaido for other Japanese
ne – isn't it?

omedeto gozaimasu – congratulations
oni-san – elder brother, also used to show respect to other young males

onna-zuki – a ladies' man (lit. 'likes women')
ossan – old git
otsukare sama deshita – thanks for your hard work

pachinko – a form of gambling often called Japanese pinball, but more closely resembling a vertical version of bagatelle
Pil Sung Corea – Victory to Korea (Korean)

rakki – lucky
ramen – noodles, originally from China, served in a large bowl with soup and various accompaniments

saiko – brilliant, excellent, the best
sashimi – usually raw fish, though sometimes raw whale, beef, horse or chicken meat
sayonara – goodbye
Self-Defence Forces – the Japanese military
sempai – senior, a term of respect
sento – public baths, for washing not swimming
shacho – company owner or president
shinjinrui – new species
shoganai – it can't be helped
shotengai – covered shopping street or arcade
snack – a bar where customers are entertained by hostesses
soapland – a kind of 'massage' where a woman uses her body to wash a man's

ureshii – happy

wasabi – ground horseradish

yaki bibimba – Korean dish made from rice, vegetables, mince, *kimchi* and chili sauce, mixed in pre-heated stone bowls
yokatta – that's good

zannen – that's a shame